Humanitarian Logistics: A New Field of Research and Action

Humanitarian Logistics: A New Field of Research and Action

Aruna Apte

*Naval Postgraduate School
Monterey CA, 93943
USA
auapte@nps.edu*

now

the essence of knowledge

Boston – Delft

Foundations and Trends® in Technology, Information and Operations Management

Published, sold and distributed by:
now Publishers Inc.
PO Box 1024
Hanover, MA 02339
USA
Tel. +1-781-985-4510
www.nowpublishers.com
sales@nowpublishers.com

Outside North America:
now Publishers Inc.
PO Box 179
2600 AD Delft
The Netherlands
Tel. +31-6-51115274

The preferred citation for this publication is A. Apte, Humanitarian Logistics: A New Field of Research and Action, Foundation and Trends® in Technology, Information and Operations Management, vol 3, no 1, pp 1–100, 2009

ISBN: 978-1-60198-336-7
© 2010 A. Apte

All rights reserved. No part of this publication may be reproduced, stored in a retrieval system, or transmitted in any form or by any means, mechanical, photocopying, recording or otherwise, without prior written permission of the publishers.

Photocopying. In the USA: This journal is registered at the Copyright Clearance Center, Inc., 222 Rosewood Drive, Danvers, MA 01923. Authorization to photocopy items for internal or personal use, or the internal or personal use of specific clients, is granted by now Publishers Inc for users registered with the Copyright Clearance Center (CCC). The 'services' for users can be found on the internet at: www.copyright.com

For those organizations that have been granted a photocopy license, a separate system of payment has been arranged. Authorization does not extend to other kinds of copying, such as that for general distribution, for advertising or promotional purposes, for creating new collective works, or for resale. In the rest of the world: Permission to photocopy must be obtained from the copyright owner. Please apply to now Publishers Inc., PO Box 1024, Hanover, MA 02339, USA; Tel. +1-781-871-0245; www.nowpublishers.com; sales@nowpublishers.com

now Publishers Inc. has an exclusive license to publish this material worldwide. Permission to use this content must be obtained from the copyright license holder. Please apply to now Publishers, PO Box 179, 2600 AD Delft, The Netherlands, www.nowpublishers.com; e-mail: sales@nowpublishers.com

Foundations and Trends® in Technology, Information and Operations Management

Volume 3 Issue 1, 2009

Editorial Board

Editor-in-Chief:
Uday Karmarkar
Times Mirror Chair in Management Strategy & Policy
The Anderson School at UCLA
Los Angeles, California 90095-1418
USA
uday.karmarkar@anderson.ucla.edu

Editors

Uday Apte (Southern Methodist University)
Rajiv Banker (Temple University)
Gabriel Bitran (MIT)
Roger Bohn (UC San Diego)
Gerard Cachon (University of Pennsylvania)
Morris Cohen (University of Pennsylvania)
Sriram Dasu (University of Southern California)
Awi Federgruen (Columbia University)
Marshall Fisher (University of Pennsylvania)
Art Geoffrion (UCLA)
Steve Graves (MIT)
Vijay Gurbaxani (UC Irvine)
Wallace J. Hopp (Northwestern University)
Ananth Iyer (Purdue University)
Sunder Kekre (Carnegie Mellon University)
Ton de Kok (Technical University Eindhoven)
Panos Kouvelis (Washington University)
Christoph Loch (INSEAD)
Haim Mendelson (Stanford University)
Mohanbir Sawhney (Northwestern University)
Avi Seidman (University of Rochester)
Josep Valor (IESE Business School)
Jo van Nunen (Erasmus University)
Garrett van Ryzin (Columbia University)
Luk van Wassenhove (INSEAD)
Andrew Whinston (University of Texas, Austin)
Candice Yano (UC Berkeley)

Editorial Scope

Foundations and Trends® in Technology, Information and Operations Management will publish survey and tutorial articles in the following topics:

- B2B Commerce
- Business Process Engineering and Design
- Business Process Outsourcing
- Capacity Planning
- Competitive Operations
- Contracting in Supply Chains
- E-Commerce and E-Business Models
- Electronic markets, auctions and exchanges
- Enterprise Management Systems
- Facility Location
- Information Chain Structure and Competition
- International Operations
- Marketing/Manufacturing Interfaces
- Multi-location inventory theory
- New Product & Service Design
- Queuing Networks
- Reverse Logistics
- Service Logistics and Product Support
- Supply Chain Management
- Technology Management and Strategy
- Technology, Information and Operations in:
  - Automotive Industries
  - Electronics manufacturing
  - Financial Services
  - Health Care
  - Industrial Equipment
  - Media and Entertainment
  - Process Industries
  - Retailing
  - Telecommunications

Information for Librarians

Foundations and Trends® in Technology, Information and Operations Management, 2009, Volume 3, 4 issues. ISSN paper version 1571-9545. ISSN online version 1571-9553. Also available as a combined paper and online subscription.

Humanitarian Logistics: A New Field of Research and Action

Aruna Apte

Graduate School of Business and Public Policy, Naval Postgraduate School, 555 Dyer Road, Monterey CA, 93943, USA, auapte@nps.edu

Abstract

Recent natural disasters such as the earthquake in Haiti, Hurricane Katrina in the United States, tsunami in the Indian Ocean, the earthquake in Pakistan, and numerous humanitarian challenges arising from such conflicts as that in Sudan have exposed the shortcomings in planning for disasters. In addition to the natural disasters, the homeland security issues related to domestic as well as international terrorism have increased the fear factor and have made 'readiness' the principal priority. Humanitarian logistics is a critical element of an effective disaster relief process. The objective of this monograph is to discuss research issues and potential actions surrounding the new field of humanitarian logistics. We define humanitarian logistics as that special branch of logistics which manages response supply chain of critical supplies and services with challenges such as demand surges, uncertain supplies, critical time windows in face of infrastructure vulnerabilities and vast scope and size of the operations. We survey case studies to learn from the past experience and review analytical models from the literature to understand the state-of-the-art in humanitarian logistics. We recommend further research in the fields of operations management and operations research to improve the effectiveness and efficiency of humanitarian logistics. We conclude that though humanitarian logistics is inherently chaotic and complex, and it is difficult to do research in this area, the complexity and obstacles can be dealt with by the researchers.

Keywords: Humanitarian; logistics; disaster; emergency; relief; response; supply chain; analytical models; prepositioning; facility location; distribution; evacuation; inventory; decision making.

Contents

1 Introduction 1

2 Humanitarian Logistics 5
2.1 The Need 6
2.2 Lessons Learned 9
2.3 Disaster Classification 12
2.4 Disaster Response and Humanitarian Relief 15

3 Design of Humanitarian Logistics 17
3.1 Military, Commercial and Humanitarian Logistics: A Comparison 18
3.2 Supply Chain Considerations 20
3.3 Humanitarian Logistics as a Supply Chain 26

4 Supply Chain Issues in Humanitarian Logistics 29
4.1 Preparation 31
4.2 Disaster Response 45
4.3 Relief Operations 58

5 Organizational Issues in Humanitarian Logistics 67
5.1 Collaboration 67
5.2 Information and Knowledge Management 69

5.3	Training and Education	70
5.4	Role of Donors and Donations	70
5.5	Risk Management	71

6 Conclusions and Potential for Future Research   73

6.1	Examples of Actual Practice	73
6.2	Challenges Today in Humanitarian Logistics	78
6.3	Future Research	84

Acknowledgements   89

References   91

1

Introduction

A significant proportion of the world's population has suffered in recent years as a result of disasters — both natural and manmade. Humanitarian responses to the 2004 tsunami in the Indian Ocean, the 2005 earthquake in Pakistan, various hurricanes in the United States, the conflict in Sudan, and the spread of HIV/AIDS in Africa have largely been neither effective nor efficient. A recent example of this is the 2010 earthquake in Haiti and the devastation after that. The reasons are many, but are partly attributable to the sheer size and scope of such disasters. As reported by the Center for Research on the Epidemiology of the Disaster (CRED), between 1974 and 2003 there were 6,637 natural disasters worldwide that affected 5.1 billion people and accrued $1.38 trillion (US$) in damage [56]. In 2007 alone, 106 natural disasters killed 17,000 people and affected 201 million more [107]. Between May and September 2007, the Red Cross responded to natural disasters in 18 countries in Africa, 16 in the Americas, 13 in Asia, and 10 in European Nations [69].

As a result of the Indian Ocean tsunami in 2004, the overall budgets for humanitarian efforts have increased — and this in turn has brought increased attention to humanitarian logistics. It is commonly agreed that disaster relief has a large logistics component [82, 162, 164]. With the 2004 budgets of the top 10 humanitarian agencies exceeding $14 billion in total, the logistics of aid has attracted recent scrutiny [155]. Consequently, humanitarian logistics has become a topic of interest to both academics and practitioners [82]. An effective and efficient humanitarian response depends "on the ability of logisticians to procure, transport and receive supplies at the site of a humanitarian relief effort" [153].

The objective of this monograph is to take a comprehensive look at the issues surrounding humanitarian logistics through the life cycle of the disaster spanning three stages of operations: preparation, disaster response, and humanitarian relief. We define humanitarian logistics from different perspectives, survey case studies to delineate lessons learned, and review analytical models from the literature to understand the state-of-the-art in humanitarian logistics. We then recommend further research in the fields of operations management and operations research to improve the effectiveness and efficiency of humanitarian logistics.

This monograph consists of six sections, including the current introductory section. In the next section, we review various aspects of humanitarian logistics to provide a comprehensive definition. We discuss the need for humanitarian logistics, review the lessons learned in past humanitarian logistics efforts, develop a classification of disasters, and distinguish between disaster response and humanitarian relief. In Section 3 we discuss the factors important for the design of humanitarian logistics using traditional concepts of logistics and supply chain management. Specifically, we compare humanitarian logistics with the military logistics as well as commercial supply chains.

Sections 4 and 5 describe supply chain issues and organizational issues in humanitarian logistics. In Section 4 we review analytical models related to humanitarian logistics. In reviewing analytical models we focus on efficiency and effectiveness of various aspects of humanitarian logistics. This review includes models that have been published in extant research literature as well as those that have been proposed in various working papers known to the author. We should point out that although this monograph is intended for all audiences, academics as well as practitioners, the academic community may find the discussion of analytical models in Section 4 particularly useful in their research efforts. Section 5 discusses organizational issues, such as collaboration among players, flow of information, knowledge management, etc., that are important factors in humanitarian logistics. Motivation for discussing the literature in these two sections is to present an informal survey of the current research.

In Section 6, the last section, we present case studies of current practices to place this academic research in the context of reality. We believe this will provide the broader picture of humanitarian logistics. In the same section we also describe the challenges as seen by the officials in the field. The case studies combined with challenges highlight the research needed in humanitarian logistics, a new field of research and action.

2

Humanitarian Logistics

Response to a disaster must be tailored to the characteristics of the disaster. A disaster is defined by Federal Emergency Management Agency (FEMA) as an event that causes 100 deaths or 100 human injuries or damage worth US$ 1 million. Preparing for a humanitarian response predominantly involves managing the logistics of potential responses [156, 164]. In order to better understand this process, we must define humanitarian logistics. To this end, in this section we first explain the need for logistics. Furthermore, in order to understand humanitarian logistics we also need to understand disasters. Hence we present a classification of disasters based on time and location. We then review the lessons learned so far to gauge the scope of humanitarian logistics. Finally, we distinguish between disaster response and humanitarian relief to establish the definition of humanitarian logistics.

The term, "Logistics," has different meanings to different organizations and people. The goal of operational logistics in the military, for example, is to sustain military operations and bridging the gap between strategic logistics (e.g., national stockpiles, industrial infrastructure, and power-projection capabilities) and tactical logistics (e.g., unit-level sustainment) [83]. In the business sector, logistics is defined as a "planning framework for the management of material, service, information, and capital flows and includes the increasingly complex information, material, communication, and control systems required in today's business environment" [164]. In contrast, most humanitarian organizations such as the World Food Program (WFP) and Medicines Sans Frontiers (MSF) agree that humanitarian logistics is "the process of planning, implementing, and controlling the efficient, cost-effective, flow and storage of goods and materials, as well as related information, from point of origin to point of consumption for the purpose of meeting the end beneficiary's requirements" [154]. In maintaining and increasing efficiency and effectiveness of this logistics, one important fact to remember is that the three principles of "humanitarian space", humanity, neutrality, and impartiality, have to be present during the strategic, tactical, and operational stages of humanitarian operations [158].

2.1 The Need

History and research suggest that humanitarian logistics should be more evidence-based. One of the ways to verify is if resources allocated for planning or responding to any disaster are justified by data. However, "Data on disaster occurrence, their effect upon people and cost to countries remain at best patchy" [56]. The key sources of such data in recent years have been insurance companies as well as specialized agencies such as the World Food Program (WFP) and the World Health Organization (WHO). The recent increase in the occurrence of disasters shown in Figure 2.1 can possibly be explained by the increase over time in the reporting of small disasters. Other plausible reason is the population increase fueled by migration to disaster prone areas.

Similar to under-reporting of disaster occurrences, the details regarding economic losses are also frequently under-reported. Difficulties in arriving at accurate estimates of economic loss and the absence of internationally accepted methods of damage assessment [56] are partly responsible for the lack of data on economic losses caused by disasters. In any event, the devastating effect of disasters on economies and human health has prompted investigations into the underlying causes and their remedy resulting in the need for humanitarian logistics. For example, one such remedy in reducing human suffering in

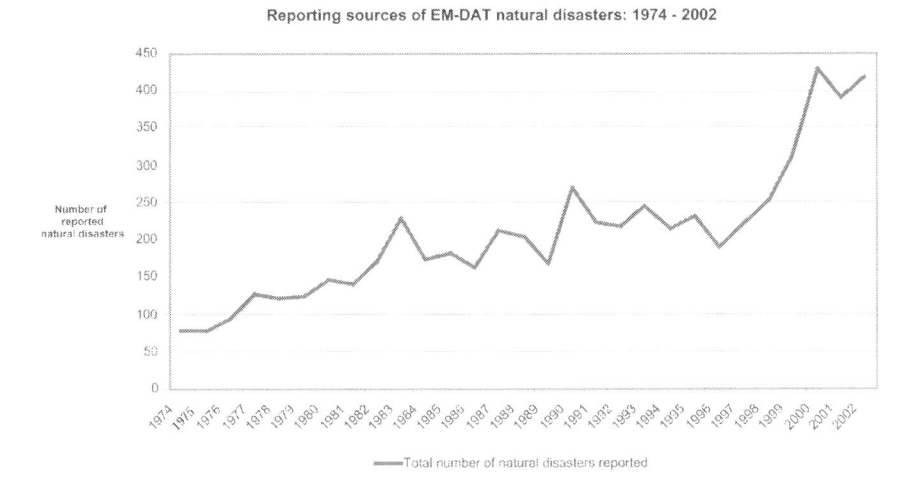

Fig. 2.1 Natural disasters 1974–2003 (*Source*: Guha-Sapir et al., [56]).

natural disasters is to proactively prepare for and pre-position supplies in best possible locations. Economy of the affected area depends on transportation, so one solution may be securing infrastructure issues through long-term actions. These strategic issues in logistics are major challenges in face of funding problems.

But humanitarian agencies face a number of operational challenges as well. For example, though their primary mission is to respond to disasters as they occur, humanitarian agencies must also satisfy their donors, without whose substantial pledges the affected communities could not be served [115, 164]. Additionally, many of the distributed supplies are donations received to the humanitarian agencies instead of being purchased directly by them. As a result, humanitarian agencies have the additional task of managing donated supplies which may or may not be necessary or suitable for the given disaster. The problems experienced with the suitability of donated supplies in case of the Pakistan earthquake in 2005 are presented in Exhibit 1. Humanitarian agencies must streamline the in-flow of donations so that "differing or overlapping aid" do not result in "oversupply or inappropriate supply" [107]. The need to suitably handle genetically modified food, about-to-expire medications, and substantial amounts of unused supplies create further challenges.

Exhibit 1: Pakistan Earthquake (2005)

> Greg Mortensen, the best-selling author of *Three Cups of Tea*, has worked extensively in Pakistan and Afghanistan for humanitarian purposes such as building schools. After the Pakistan earthquake he noticed women burning fancy tweed jackets as fuel for cooking food. It seemed there was enough warm clothing to go around but no fuel for cooking.
>
> The tents donated by kind individuals for shelter came with no instructions. And in some instances, even if the instructions were there, most of the victims could not understand the language. Folks did not know how to put those tents up. Moreover, some key pieces were missing. After resolving all the issues when the tents were up, large families gathered in one tent around the fire to stay warm. The tents caught fire and instead of being any help they became a deadly hazard.

Source: Mortensen [111].

According to the Munich Reinvestment group, the real annual economic losses have grown from US$75.5 billion in 1960s to US$659.9 billion in the 1990s. The forecasts are for five fold increases in the number of natural and manmade disasters in the next 50 years [155]. In light of this, the field of humanitarian logistics is gaining more interest and has seen a significant increase in research in the recent years. Although response supply chains for humanitarian causes are arguably among the "most dynamic and complex supply chains in the world" [154], proper logistics preparation before a disaster strikes can be done by coordinating processes, technologies, and communications capabilities. Such actions can improve the effectiveness and efficiency of the response supply chains, and thus that of the humanitarian agency's response. Academic research, based on input from practitioners and using operations management and operations research analysis, is critical in bridging the gap between logistical expertise and humanitarian relief. Research in areas of humanitarian relief and disaster response belongs to a special subset of the broad area of logistics.

An onslaught of recent disasters, both natural and manmade, and the fear of those that can potentially occur, have led to several research projects. The resulting articles typically discuss lessons learned, describe analytical models for humanitarian supply chain, and explore conceptual boundaries between various relief operation topics. Taken as a whole, they provide a substantial foundation for improving humanitarian logistics. For example, improved decision-making models can help humanitarian organizations and first responders refine their strategy for planning, manage their operations for prepositioning, storage and distribution, and sustain aid both during and after a crisis.

2.2 Lessons Learned

All recent disasters have had both short-term and long-term consequences, and they provide us with a wealth of lessons for the future operational planning and execution of humanitarian logistics. One of the most important lessons learned is that money is not a panacea, as evidenced in the aftermath of the tsunami in Ache, Indonesia (see Exhibit 2). The enormous quantities of food, medicine, and water that were made available as aid from outside the region (response to the disaster) could not reach the disaster victims due to non-existent distribution channels and prepositioned assets (lack of preparation) with difficulties in the last mile distribution (relief operations).

Exhibit 2: Tsunami Devastation in Banda Aceh 2004
Banda Aceh is the regional capital of Aceh, Indonesia. After the tsunami in the Indian Ocean there were enough supplies donated by the world's richest countries but there was only one airstrip and one forklift in Banda Aceh. Having available huge amounts of supplies was of less consequence since there were no means for distributing them. Money available from donations could neither be employed at the eleventh hour to build an airstrip nor to buy forklifts at the last minute. So the officials there had difficulty delivering food, water and medicines to the people who survived the disaster but needed critical commodities to carry on. In short, "the broader point is that money is not a panacea" [62].

Source: Heidtke [62], The Economist Global Agenda [152].

The horrific images of the devastation from Hurricane Katrina and the reports of how public officials failed to mitigate the resulting damage are plentiful. However, one of the lessons learned was that government officials were not the only ones ill-prepared to face that disaster. Supply chains of many manufacturers and shippers were interrupted as well. Research done by logistics managers immediately following Katrina indicates that the majority of companies had been holding far more inventory than in the previous era of "lesser inventory the better" [27]. However, despite higher inventory levels, the supply chains of these firms were not positioned to weather a disaster of such magnitude. Hurricane Katrina highlighted the fact that logistics managers must consider a multitude of factors relevant to their supply chain, including developing a contingency plan for warehouse locations, forecasting demand to estimate the amount of inventory to be held, determining the appropriate amount of flexibility in their distribution channels, etc. Whether to hold more inventories to reduce lead time or not protect against destruction is something that can be learned from the past. However, such decisions are further complicated by the fact that the more global the supply chain, the more difficult are the contingency planning, humanitarian efforts, transportation, and distribution.

In a response supply chain, delivery during the last mile is always an issue. When Telegraph was developed over a century ago, it revolutionized the way people communicated. Although it was a major technological breakthrough, the system still required a runner to deliver the actual message from the local telegraph office to the ultimate recipient — a requirement known as the 'last mile problem.' Today, the humanitarian agencies are facing the same last mile distribution problem: how to deliver the right supplies to the right population at the right time? Frequently, the supplies are plentiful but they cannot be effectively deployed because of logistical problems in the response supply chain. For this last phase of humanitarian aid, scheduling of deliveries, routing of delivery vehicles, effectively managed supply inventory, and efficient transportation of these supplies play a crucial roles in this response.

Studies in logistics conclude that infrastructure such as distribution centers, warehouses, and medical clinics should be established in locations based on proximity to high-population areas and transportation hubs. Facility location is of utmost importance for distribution of critical supplies and services under uncertainty.

In addition to location of distribution centers, for the last mile distribution, warehousing strategies involving prepositioning of needed supplies is also important in many other complex humanitarian logistics systems. One such lesson learned was through the response to continued humanitarian relief for the millions of displaced people in South Sudan (a first quadrant disaster). The United Nations Children's Fund (UNICEF) established Operation Lifeline Sudan (OLS) to operate and provide airlifts of food and critical supplies from Lochichoggio, Kenya. Because of presence of OLS and the security it offers, many non-governmental organizations (NGOs) pre-positioned relief items in the warehouses there. Here the inventory management played an important role in warehousing [15] in terms of order quantities, reorder points, and types of demand.

However, even with sound prepositioning, warehousing, inventory management, transportation, and last mile distribution, the unexpected surges and the diversity of demand require the processes to be agile to ensure that the aid can reduce the victim suffering. "Rapid deployment on demand" [164] is an essential strategy that can lead to successful humanitarian relief effort.

In addition to the deployment of supplies and services, another lesson learned due to the evacuation fiasco after Hurricane Katrina in the United States is rapid mass evacuation planning. Unfortunately, during Katrina, "beginning with the evacuation orders before the hurricane landfall, some public officials did not know what those right steps might be" [114]. Some of the lessons learned here are that there exist specific vulnerabilities of evacuees such as race and culture [38]. It also suggests the need for evacuation planning [8, 114, 138, 167].

Mass evacuation is not possible if there is no coordination, co-operation, and collaboration amongst parties involved. This can be accomplished through the network of community-based volunteers and staff members. It is essential not just for evacuation but for supporting all stages of the humanitarian logistics, planning, deployment, and recovery effort. One of the major lessons learned from recent disasters is that without the collaboration between partners — internal and external to the system, military and civilian, private sector and non-profit organizations — execution of disaster response is likely to be far from adequate. In fact, without such collaboration humanitarian operations may be derailed by a "multiplicity of agencies and governments" [135].

Such efforts from staff members and especially volunteers of humanitarian agencies cannot be efficient if the personnel involved are not trained properly. The need for training and education of first responders has been demonstrated in various crises. In addition, standards must be developed "to ensure that emergency planning, field operations and personnel training are conducted rigorously" [2]. In order to appreciate these outcomes and act on them in the future we need to understand this process of humanitarian logistics for which we first need to understand disasters.

2.3 Disaster Classification

Disasters can be classified based on the specific characteristics of disasters including the speed of onset, slow or sudden; and the source of disaster, natural or manmade [43, 164]. It is customary to classify disasters as natural versus manmade. Especially since between 1982 and 1994, 97% of humanitarian operations were devoted to disaster relief for manmade disasters [164]. However, the funding typically flows to the disaster that gets media exposure or strikes a nerve. The level of resources available in responding to such manmade disasters can be significantly different. Malice and intelligence in planning make manmade disasters difficult to anticipate and hence problematic for humanitarians agencies in several respects, such as safety and security, in addition to basic logistics operations. Yet, a classification based on manmade versus natural disasters does not achieve substantial inference for research in terms of operations. In either case it is a disaster which needs to be responded to. Therefore we do not focus on this type of classification.

Using the level of difficulty potentially present in humanitarian operations as the criteria we classify disasters based on time and location. This is illustrated in Figure 2.2. Based on this classification we can determine the factors that play important roles in disaster response or humanitarian relief. This is not to say that providing aid in case of localized slow-onset disaster is always easy but level of difficulty is lower since it is possible to prepare for such disasters. Therefore, it helps if we also pay attention to the distinction between three stages of humanitarian logistics operations: preparation, disaster response, and ongoing humanitarian relief. We believe that preparation and prepositioning in anticipation of a disaster response, once the disaster strikes, and the on-going relief operations play a key role in determining the level of difficulty of humanitarian logistics operations.

Preparation can play an important role in the disasters classified in the first quadrant in Figure 2.2. The disasters being localized with possible lead time for preparation due to slow-onset provide this opportunity. In this case, the actual response is not likely to be that difficult since there is time to catch up and the disaster itself is geographically contained.

The second quadrant where the onset is slow but locations are dispersed, preparation can help but pre-positioning becomes challenging.

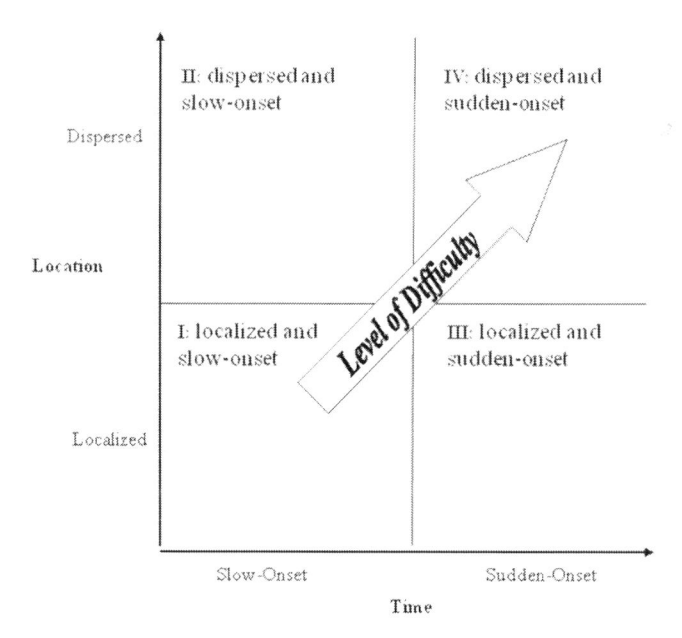

Fig. 2.2 Classification of disasters.

The large and scattered geographical area takes substantial amount of budget and coordination among players. Therefore, disaster response may play an important role here. The relief process may also pose issues due to multiple locations.

The sudden-onset disaster, even if localized, in the third quadrant creates problems in all the three roles due to obvious uncertainties. Yet, being localized, the level of operational difficulty is somewhat lower as compared to that posed in dispersed and sudden-onset disasters from the fourth quadrant.

In summary, the disasters that occur over a period of time or disasters with slow-onset provide time for humanitarians to plan and prepare for relief operations. On the other hand a disaster that strikes suddenly can pose formidable problems for response since no organization can prepare well for such event. Strategic planning such as asset prepositioning and facility location may help to some extent but the disaster response is the name of the game here. It also makes a difference in difficulty of response or relief whether the disaster is localized or if it affects large and numerous geographical areas. Effectiveness and efficiency of transportation and distribution of critical supplies and services suffer if the disasters are dispersed, such as the 2004 tsunami in the Indian Ocean which affected many countries.

Thus, the localized, slow-onset, and natural disasters (seasonal or non-seasonal) are at one end of the spectrum of the level of difficulty for humanitarian logistics whereas dispersed, sudden-onset disasters are at the other end of that spectrum. In between are the rest, for instance, localized and sudden such as 2005 hurricane Katrina in United States or the severe earthquake—magnitude 7.9 on the Richter scale — in Gujarat, India in January 2001. Though localized and sudden, there is a marked difference between these two disasters, one is seasonal and the other is not.

An influential factor in natural disasters is whether the occurrence is seasonal or non-seasonal. In the United States, tornadoes in so-called "Tornado Alley" (states such as Texas, Oklahoma, and Kansas where frequent tornadoes occur) and wildfires in California are annual events encountered in summer months. Earthquakes, on the other hand, are non-seasonal. Evacuation plans can be in place for either of the situation but will differ based on this factor. These different types of seasonal disasters, even if sometimes they are sudden, pose lesser problems than those faced in non-seasonal disasters in terms of the three key stages of humanitarian logistics. Classification of disasters and the three stages in the life cycle of a disaster suggest that we examine the similarity and distinction between disaster response and humanitarian relief.

2.4 Disaster Response and Humanitarian Relief

In a disaster response, there is immediate need for critical supplies but usually there is limited information available about the requirements. Hence, disaster response tends to become, to some extent, "reactionary logistics" [143]. Time is a distinguishing factor in disaster response since there is generally limited warning prior to the event and urgent response is needed because suffering can increase rapidly in the absence of timely aid. Humanitarian relief is an ongoing process of mitigation through disasters. It is important to note, however, that in the case of seasonal disasters it is possible to plan for the prepositioning of assets and critical supplies, and to plan for the evacuation of the affected population using information from previous disasters. Furthermore, the population affected in such sudden-onset disasters — natural or manmade — is normally concentrated in specific geographic areas. There exist exceptions to this generalization, such as the 2004 tsunami in the Indian Ocean, which affected numerous countries, and the 2008 terrorist attacks in Mumbai, India, which were widespread and simultaneous although contained in a relatively small area of the city. Disaster response also differs from humanitarian relief in that it receives comparatively more media exposure as a result of its urgency and sudden-onset.

Humanitarian relief, on the other hand, is an ongoing process for slow-onset disasters with a long-term need for supplies. To a large extent, relief requirements are known and relief organizations face relatively long planning lead times. This is not to say that these operations are easy since there are many examples where providing relief has posed numerous difficulties. Disasters such as famine in Sudan and

HIV/AIDS in Africa have affected populations in vast regions. In such cases, sustained long-term relief operations are necessary. Thus, humanitarian relief operations usually have sufficient time available in which to plan their response before the relief process begins and therefore humanitarian relief process lasts much longer than a disaster response. A consequence of the long relief process is "exposure fatigue" with the media tending to lose interest and thus limiting coverage, which ultimately results in a diminished stream of donations.

Humanitarian logistics is an integral part of both disaster response and humanitarian relief. We, in this monograph, primarily focus on disaster relief logistics and the operations within this response supply chain. We define humanitarian logistics as that special branch of logistics which manages response supply chain of critical supplies and services with challenges such as demand surges, uncertain supplies, critical time windows in face of infrastructure vulnerabilities and vast scope and size of the operations. We regard humanitarian logistics as a supply chain spanning the life cycle of a disaster. The operations in this supply chain may be loosely divided into three stages: preparation, disaster response, and ongoing humanitarian relief (sometimes known as recovery). We use this classification for discussing supply chain issues in humanitarian logistics throughout the monograph but more specifically in the fourth section.

3

Design of Humanitarian Logistics

In this section we discuss issues related to the design of humanitarian logistics. We do this by first understanding the differences and similarities between military, commercial, and humanitarian logistics. We then frame the humanitarian logistics as the response supply chain by describing various components and characteristics. We distinguish logistics decisions at three levels of decision making: strategic, tactical, and operational. Decisions made at the strategic level, such as research and development of logistical capabilities, sourcing of supplies, determination of distribution policies, and build up of physical infrastructure, have long-lasting impacts [83]. Two important strategic issues for humanitarian logistics are the building and maintenance of infrastructure and the prepositioning of assets and critical supplies. These issues also encompass technological capabilities, inventory support for warehouses full of consumable and non-consumable supplies, building or maintaining roads, bridges and airstrips. At the strategic level, humanitarian logistics can be managed well if sufficient experience has been gained from prior disasters and if sufficient funds are available. The objective here is to develop capabilities and infrastructure to reduce suffering while being cost-effective in disasters.

At the operational level, decisions pertain to the end-game being played out in the affected areas. This stage of humanitarian logistics potentially entails for example, evacuations of the affected population or the last mile distribution of critical supplies and services, executed with specificity and customization. An important operational detail is applying such customization to supply inventory. The objective of operational decision is to get relief to the affected population, quickly.

Tactical decisions in humanitarian logistics bridge the functional gap between the strategic and operational levels. At this level, decisions are made about gathering resources (inventory management) and then transporting and deploying them as needed. The primary objective at the tactical level is the real-time management of the supply chain, with optimal inventory, routing, distribution, and scheduling of delivery of the supplies, while keeping in mind that the supplies should be delivered as soon as possible.

Analytical tools can be extremely useful in optimizing this response supply chain at all levels. For example, models at strategic level for resource allocation, and facility location; at tactical level for inventory management, distribution and scheduling; and at operational level for evacuation, lead time reduction and last mile distribution. This topic is discussed at length later in the monograph.

3.1 Military, Commercial and Humanitarian Logistics: A Comparison

According to U.S. Field Manual 100-16 [35], "military logistics is the process of planning and executing the movement and sustainment of operating forces in the execution of military strategy and operations." It is the foundation of combat power — the bridge that connects the nation's industrial base to its operating forces. This definition can be further modified to, "a discipline that encompasses the resources that are needed to keep the means of the military process (operation) going in order to achieve its desired outputs (objectives). Logistics includes planning, managing, tracking and controlling these resources" [83].

As reflected in much of the literature, military logistics is regarded by many as a quantitative discipline. From this perspective, the parameters of logistics include amounts of fuel for ship and aircraft, ordnance, consumable and non-consumable goods, and time windows such as force accumulation time, order-to-ship time, scheduling time [22] and many more. There are, of course, many other important logistics issues that are difficult to quantify such as collaboration, information and knowledge management, education, and training. Such issues are unaccounted for by the quantitative analysis. In the rest of the section we focus on quantitative aspects of military and humanitarian logistics.

Many of the challenges in commercial logistics management [18, pp. 3–6] are also reflected in military and humanitarian logistics. However, there are some significant differences. For example, in commercial logistics, the distribution network is reconfigured by management if they deem it necessary to meet changes in demand patterns. Although demand patterns and demand locations change only occasionally in commercial enterprises, they change frequently within the context of conflict and disaster. Thus, the configuration of a distribution network may be anchored but the last mile distribution is necessarily dynamic and uncertain for military and also for humanitarian logistics.

Furthermore, while managing inventory is problematic in the retail environment, it is even more complex in military logistics due to the distance between locations of commodities and troops. In case of disaster response same problem is prevalent. For example, inventory management of prophylaxis for a pandemic is major issue faced by the controlling agency, such as the Federal Emergency Management Agency (FEMA) or the Centers for Disease Control and Prevention (CDC). As a result of instability and uncertainty, concerns about issues of fleet management, packing, routing, and delivery of supplies within specified time windows are compounded during times of disaster and conflict. Military and humanitarian logistics have significant commonalities across many of these issues.

Military (especially in the United States) has typically played an important role in providing support during disasters. Military has an underlying reliable structure for command and control. This structure is critical in case of chaotic situation such as war or disaster. Humanitarian logistics would benefit from military support for ensuring effectiveness. Setting aside political and security reasons, the commonality of situation in war and disaster in conjunction with structure and resource acquisition in military logistics may help explain why military support during disasters is often more effective than other forms of aid (except for certain commercial organizations such as Wal-Mart).

As per funding, military mission normally dictates accomplishment despite the cost. This does not mean that budget is not a consideration but supporting of the mission is preferred over saving money. If the mission is necessary then the funds are made available. Unfortunately, this may or may not happen in humanitarian logistics since acquisition of resources is dependent on donations.

3.2 Supply Chain Considerations

A supply chain in its most basic form encompasses three elements: supply, demand, and flow — flow being the intermediary between the other two components. In general, a commercial supply chain supplies a pre-established, standardized product to customers to meet a relatively constant and forecasted demand via structured resources and continuous flow. In contrast, at any given time, a response supply chain in humanitarian logistics supplies a wide range of products and services fulfilling spurts of demand while sharing the flow and capacity with other relief items [44].

Many businesses believe that making their supply chains faster and more cost-effective gives them a competitive edge. However, "Only companies that build supply chains that are agile, adaptive and aligned get ahead of their rivals" [90]. The supply chain for humanitarian relief must be agile [115], i.e., be able to respond to abruptly changing supply and demand, and must also be adaptive to market and strategy changes. For example, when a disaster strikes, information may not be immediately available to define accurate requirements for the affected population — and subsequent information may make the initial prepositioning strategy inappropriate or obsolete. Throughout this supply chain, from the source to the donors and finally to the customers (the affected population), the common goal is relief. All the nodes in between — producers, distributors, and humanitarian agencies — need to be aligned to achieve that goal. Since the supply chain for humanitarian relief and disaster response exists out of necessity, one might conclude that agility, adaptability, and alignment [90] are particularly critical for the humanitarian logistics. Unfortunately, although agreement exists amongst humanitarian logisticians about the need for the alignment of agents in a supply chain, such alignment is difficult to achieve when the agents consist of a mix of non-profit organizations, for-profit businesses, and government entities.

The following are factors common to both commercial supply chains and humanitarian logistics viewed as a supply chain:

- Supply
- Inventory
- Distribution Network
- Flows
- Lead Time
- Information System
- Customer
- Demand

In addition, factors such as the organization's objective and performance measures, and agility, adaptability, and alignment can further define the supply chain. We now discuss each of these factors from the perspective of both types of supply chains.

Supply: To meet customer demands, the supplier provides the product in the quantity needed by customer. In a commercial supply chain, the demand has at least two characteristics: the specification of the product is usually clear and the demand distribution, if not the forecasted demand, is also reasonably known. However, in a humanitarian logistics (unless it is in response to a slow-onset disaster), the relief items in demand, though from a small list, are diverse in kind and quantity. The suppliers of these items, other than the ones with whom contracts already exist, are also not always known in advance. The suppliers could consist of one or more vendors, donors, or a combination thereof. "Donations place additional complications on the procurement process, since it is difficult to define what will come from donors, and what will have to be secured from vendors" [44]. Furthermore, donors usually do not have comprehensive information about the relief organization's existing inventory. The ambiguity and uncertainty of supply pose a major challenge for humanitarian logistics.

Inventory: With reasonable predictability of demand and inventory visibility, inventory control is manageable in commercial supply chains. Absent these factors, inventory control can be extremely difficult in supply chains for humanitarian purposes [104]. Moreover, any long delivery time for supplies during a disaster resulting sometimes in outages forces high inventory levels. An inventory management policy could be developed by the humanitarian organization to assure a steady stream of supplies from warehouses to its points of distribution. Depending on the type of disaster and the shelf life of supplies, storage may be either short term or long term. For example, in the 1989 relief efforts in South Sudan, supplies such as grains had to be held for long periods of time [15]. But in the case of a pandemic, such as bird flu, the vaccines have a short shelf life. Perishability of the vaccine and its obsolescence due to a change in virus strain both contribute toward a short shelf life. Such supply issues complicate the inventory management system, particularly in humanitarian logistics.

Distribution Network: In a crisis, when the infrastructure is at risk, transportation and distribution become a significant issue. In cases of earthquake or flood, roads may not be traversable and the already challenging last mile distribution in the supply chain becomes an even greater hurdle. The location of the disaster may further complicate supply distribution, as observed in the aftermath of the 2005 Pakistan earthquake due to geography and politics. The methods and vehicles of distribution generally available in commercial supply chains become a luxury in a disaster situation.

Flow: The flow of products in most commercial supply chain is managed so as to create a match between demand and supply. However, due to the large uncertainty around the acquisition of supplies, unknown demand, and vulnerable infrastructure, the flow of products in a supply chain for humanitarian response can be anything but smooth.

Lead Time: In a disaster, the ideal lead time of relief supplies from the victims' perspective is zero, but the same disaster can induce longer lead times for the humanitarian organizations. Here, although there exists a need for reliable supply of different products with substantially smaller lead time, due to lack of information on requirements, the humanitarian relief supply chain may not be able to mimic its commercial counterpart. It is interesting to note that certain commercial organizations such as Wal-Mart and Waffle-house were very effective in responding to hurricane Katrina disaster in the United States. The humanitarian response supply chain can learn from the operational practices of these commercial organizations.

Information System: Supply chains for humanitarian causes have several systemic deficiencies, one of which is ineffective leveraging of information technology [155]. Logistics and supply chain management in the humanitarian sector is mostly a manual process. Information systems are an integral part of commercial supply chains and information management is seen as a fundamental supply chain management strategy. This characteristic is best illustrated by the well-known success of Wal-Mart, which gained phenomenal efficiencies in its supply chain through such practices as real-time tracking of inventory levels and purchases at stores, vendor managed inventory, use of RFID (radio frequency identification), etc. "Lack of existing software that can handle the dynamism of humanitarian supply chain, limited internet access, computer shortages and lack of trained staff as well as the inability of IT staff" [155] lead to inefficiencies in humanitarian supply chains.

Customer: "The issue of customer responsiveness is problematic when considering the humanitarian supply chain" [115]. The customer in this supply chain is an elusive player. On one hand, the end user from the affected population is rarely a part of the supply chain. On the other hand, the donors who provide funding or supplies must be convinced by the humanitarian organization that the victims who are in need are reached [164]. Thus in some sense donors are also customers in humanitarian logistics. Such a supply chain where the supplier and the end users are both customers who need to be pleased, presents a dichotomy that is difficult to manage.

Demand: As noted previously, demand patterns in a commercial supply chain — timeline, requirements, quantity, and location — are known with reasonable accuracy. But humanitarian organizations often lack comprehensive demand data of this type. Demand patterns are estimated, normally after the disaster strikes. The only certainty regarding this unpredictable demand is that the need is immediate. Requirements, in terms of product type, are either unknown (such as with a vaccine where the strain is not known with certainty) or are not communicated (as in the Pakistan earthquake where women burned donated tweed jackets for fuel). In addition, based on the severity of the disaster, demand quantity can be estimated, but may not be measured, and, demand locations, though known, may not be accessible.

Objective: The objective in a supply chain in humanitarian logistics is evident — to minimize "loss of life and alleviate suffering" [153]. In the commercial supply chain the strategic goal is "to produce high quality products at low cost to maximize profit and achieve high customer satisfaction" [104]. A commercial supply chain is considered successful when the bottom line profit has increased. The supply chain for humanitarian response is deemed successful when it "mitigates the urgent needs of a population with a sustainable reduction of their vulnerability in the shortest amount of time and the least amount of resources" [164]. In case of a supply chain in humanitarian logistics, although these two goals cannot be achieved simultaneously, certain tradeoffs between budget and suffering can be established.

Agility: Quick and economical responses to fluctuations in supply and demand, i.e., agility, is critical to a successful supply chain [90]. Agility is also defined as "the ability to thrive and prosper in an environment of constant and unpredictable change" [102]. In supply chains for humanitarian response, agility is essential: rapid deployment of critical supplies and services is of utmost importance in the face of unpredictable demand and uncertain supply. Although both types of supply chains should be agile, the commercial supply chain is relatively stable whereas the humanitarian response supply chain is not. Agility in humanitarian supply chain can be created by prepositioning of assets (responsiveness), quick response (efficiency), and flexibility in the face of unknown demand. This indeed is one of the strengths of humanitarian logistics "that business could use to improve their performance and competitive advantage" [164].

Adaptability: Successful commercial supply chains adapt their structure and strategies as the market evolves [90]. Without adaptability to demand, supply, and structure, the humanitarian supply chain cannot function. Supply chains for humanitarian causes must be able to set up, change structure, and modify strategies very quickly. In short, they must be adaptable.

Alignment: The correct alignment of goals of partners in a humanitarian logistics is more important than that in its commercial counterpart. Most often, a player in a commercial supply chain is looking to optimize a local function, possibly at the cost of global optimality. However, for humanitarian efforts, the effective partnership between private and humanitarian sectors, military and humanitarian organizations, and local authorities and humanitarian communities are all essential for delivering relief [158]. Though each stakeholder has multiple goals and priorities, significant inefficiencies arise when incentives are not aligned. "A supply chain works well if the risks, costs and rewards of doing business are distributed fairly across the network" [113]. Although describing a commercial supply chain, this statement is equally true for a supply chain in humanitarian logistics.

Performance Measure: A link between decision making and performance measures is fundamental to success. It is a known fact that measure of performance can drive behavior. Commercial supply chains have predominantly used two performance measures, "cost, and combination of cost and customer responsiveness" [13]. However, for humanitarian logistics, the term "cost" needs to be defined. Is the cost actual money spent or budget required or the cost to the economy? Is the cost the fatalities or suffering of the survivors or both? Cost in humanitarian logistics is some or all these based on whose perspective it is. In addition to cost as a performance measure, other measures can be applied. The typical performance measures of a commercial supply chain, resource, output, and flexibility are also good surrogates for performance measures in a supply chain for humanitarian causes [14]. If inadequate utilization of resources results in the termination of donation and funding, performance can also be measured in terms of resources. Lack of speedy deliveries shows inefficiencies. So speed could be a performance measure. If a poor relief effort leads to increased suffering and unnecessary loss of human life, then the casualties can be used as a performance measure.

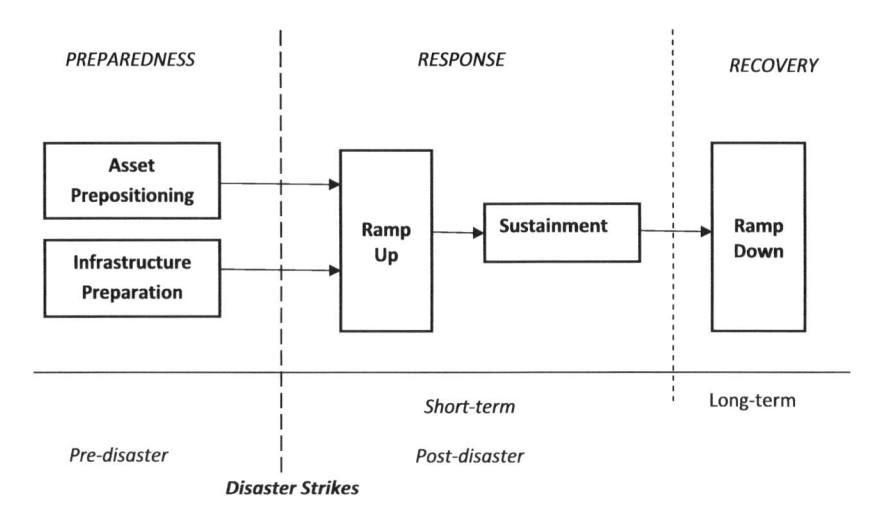

Fig. 3.1 Time line of humanitarian supply chain.

3.3 Humanitarian Logistics as a Supply Chain

Process flow in humanitarian logistics can be divided into three stages along the time line (Figure 3.1): preparedness efforts before the disaster strikes, response immediately after the disaster strikes, and recovery in the post-disaster period. The first period is strategic: the disaster has not occurred but the prepositioning of assets and infrastructure preparations take place in anticipation of a disaster [132]. Prepositioning of assets may include the expansion of warehouses, medical facilities, and temporary shelters, while infrastructure preparation may include provision of airstrips and ramp space at the airfields.

When a disaster strikes, the response follows: donations and funding are solicited from donors, supplies are obtained from pre-contracted vendors. Sometimes the supplies are obtained in advance, especially during the pre-positioning stages. The supplies received from donors and supplies purchased from vendors are then transported by various means to predetermined locations and distributed by emergency responders in the affected areas. The complexity of humanitarian logistics can be appreciated when the distribution process through this time line, along with the factors and characteristics of this supply chain are taken into account. Finally, the recovery effort is an ongoing process which must also include collecting data about lessons learned. Increasingly, to resolve some of the major issues described in this section so far, humanitarian logisticians and academics are relying on mathematical modeling, a topic we discuss next. As mentioned earlier, in the next section, we base our discussion of analytical models concerning supply chain issues in humanitarian logistics on the three natural phases of preparation, response, and recovery (relief) operations.

4

Supply Chain Issues in Humanitarian Logistics

So far we have discussed what humanitarian logistics is. First, we described the need for it. Based on lessons learned from the previous disasters we found various inadequacies which give rise to much needed research. Then we understood it in terms of a classification of different disasters. We distinguished between disaster response and humanitarian relief and compared it with military and commercial logistics to frame the supply chain issues. The design of response supply chain naturally leads to the supply chain related issues of humanitarian logistics which we now discuss in this section.

The motivation behind this discussion is to review the analytical models as they are applied to humanitarian logistics in preparation, disaster response and relief, by sampling selected articles from published and current research. The discussion in the next two sections offers the current status of the research which also reveals what has not been done. This is important for two reasons. One, the academics working in humanitarian logistics area can now place their research in the context and second, researchers wanting to work in this area can find leads to unexplored territories. From this viewpoint, in the last section of this monograph we discuss the case studies to uncover current practices, thus, divulging the complexity of strategies, their consequences, and the operations in logistics for a humanitarian cause. The informal survey in the next two sections focuses on certain elements of the response supply chain and organizational issues of the humanitarian logistics whereas the case studies offer a wider picture. The academic research and case studies offer a contrast between the specific focused issues against the broader and somewhat chaotic situations in an actual disaster. Case studies are of value especially in evaluating the implementation of academic research. The case studies in the next section highlight the research that is needed.

Until recently, emergency planners were focusing on tactical and even more on operational level of humanitarian logistics. Agility and adaptability which are vital characteristics of the humanitarian supply chain cannot be supported without being prepared or prepositioned for adequate capacity and resources. Facility location of the warehouses for resources plays an important role in this strategic pre-establishment. History and recent disasters, especially natural disasters such as Hurricane Katrina in the United States, tsunami in the Indian Ocean, typhoons in Bangladesh "beg the questions: What assets need to be in place in anticipation of a disaster? And, where should they be located?" [132]. After locating the facilities and prepositioning the assets, inventories of critical supplies must be managed well. Distribution of these supplies and dispensing of services are equally important since last mile distribution is an inherent hazard in a supply chain. Transporting the critical supplies and personnel from source to affected areas, evacuation of all types of individuals to temporary or permanent shelters and medical facilities wherever necessary play major roles in the humanitarian logistics. A decision support system in place encompassing all these aspects of the supply chain facilitates reach of the first responders and avoids fiasco.

From the perspective of the key stages in humanitarian logistics, preparation, disaster response, and relief, we now proceed to discuss the supply chain issues that influence the research and action in humanitarian logistics. Preparation includes problems such as facility location, pre-positioning of assets, resource allocation, and planning for transportation in anticipation of disaster. The actual disaster response includes problems of inventory management, distribution, and decision making during the crisis. Amongst these issues, inventory management is a concern across all these time lines of before, during, and after with different supplies needed at different time. The issue of relief includes transportation, evacuation, traffic management, and such.

Some of the approaches mentioned above have been applied to military logistics and to commercial supply chain but we focus on problems from humanitarian logistics angle. Here humanitarian and logistics both are key words. For example facility location for prepositioning is part of logistics and emergency services are a substantial part of humanitarian effort. Therefore, we focus on facility location of emergency services but not just emergency services.

Though the research reviewed is categorized based on these three stages of humanitarian logistics, preparation, disaster response, and ongoing relief, there clearly exists a crossover between these articles. Locating facilities sometimes also refers to level of inventory and so does distribution. Distribution also involves transportation and relief operations include delivery of commodities as well as evacuation. Therefore this arrangement is more for guidance than categorization.

4.1 Preparation

Preparation in anticipation of a disaster involves prepositioning of assets and resource allocation. A significant part of it involves location of warehouses, distribution centers, and so forth. At the other end of the spectrum, it involves planning for vehicle replacement. We focus on these issues in this subsection. Though inventory management, especially what to store, where to store, and when to store are important issues in planning they are also part of disaster response. We therefore discuss inventory management in the next subsection.

4.1.1 Facility Location

Prepositioning of critical supplies and services has been researched using, predominantly, two types of optimization models, set covering problem (SCP) and facility location problem (FLP). In a set covering problem each facility is associated with a region and it is strictly a binary problem asking a question does one build/locate or not. There is no "how to build/locate" involved in it. The facility location problem is a network-based problem where one chooses a facility from a candidate list making the decision which facility to close or open and sometimes which one to expand. Both the models decide upon location but address different issues. Traditionally, the latter is known as an FLP in the context of distribution networks or supply chains. Some of the research in facility location and prepositioning discussed below is summarized in terms of major decision and objective of the model, and the method in Table 4.1.

Emergency planners often must deal with design or reconfiguration of disaster systems. Number of approaches developed by researchers are based on optimization problems such as minimum cost maximal covering problems known as location set covering problem (LSCP). The objective function typically minimizes the number of facilities required. LSCP, since then has been extended to problems where instead of distance, coverage time is used. LSCP also requires covering all demand points which may not be realistic in face of budgets. Maximal Covering Location Problem (MCLP) does not require the coverage of all demand points due to limited budget which is modeled as a constraint of placing "p" facilities to maximize coverage. In the past, Brandeau and Chiu [19] provided a broad overview of over 50 representative problems in location research. Klose and Drexl [79] describe the current state-of-the-art facility location models for distribution system design.

Determining good locations of facilities with special attention to "maximum time or distance that separates a user from his closest service", dates back to the article by Toregas et al. [161]. This model is most applicable to locations of emergency service facilities such as fire stations though it can easily represent schools or libraries. There have been various modifications of MCLP model as reviewed extensively by Marianov and ReVelle [97] for emergency services. Locating emergency services is critical in preparing for disasters and there has been significant work done dealing with this issue [26, 49, 59, 150, 161].

An interesting example for locating emergency services is of basing Airtankers for forest fire control in Ontario, Canada [96]. The problem

Table 4.1. Summary of Literature Facility Location and prepositioning of assets.

Article	Major decision	Objective	Method
Balcik and Beamon [10]	Number and locations of distributing centers in a relief network	Maximize total expected demand coverage	Maximal covering location model integrating facility location and inventory decision
Cataldi et al. [24]	Location of distributing facilities and deployment plan	Maximize reduction in Maleria risk	Optimization model, solved with heuristics
Dekle et al. [33]	Identify potential disaster recovery centers	Minimize total number of disaster relief centers for each county residence within a given distance	Covering Location Problem with a two-stage approach
Duran [36]	Given initial investment find the network congiguration	Minimize average response time	Prepositioning model
Hale and Moberg [60]	Establish an efficient network of secure storage facilities	Minimize number of sites supporting multiple supply chain facilities	Location Set Covering Problem
Lee et al. [88]	Number of dispensing sites	Minimize number of points of dispensing (POD)	Facility location model
McCall [105]	Identify preposition locations for pack-up kits	Minimize "victim-nautical-miles" to transport kits to each disaster location	Location mixed-integer programming model
Ozdamar et al. [119]	Logistic plan indicating optimal mixed pick up and delivery schedules along with optimal quantities and types of loads picked up and delivered on the routes	Minimize unstatisfied demand	Hybrid of multi-commodity network flow and vehicle routing problem
Rawls and Turnquist [126]	Location of emergency supplies and allocating quantities of those supplies	Minimize expected costs over all scenarios	Two-stage stochastic optimization model influenced by facility location and resource allocation
Salmeron and Apte [132]	First stage decisions for expansion of resources and second stage for logistics	Minimized expected number of casualties and then expected number of people left behind	Two-stage stochastic optimization model
Tean [151]	Prepositioning decisions for resources	Maximize expected rescued survivors and delivery of commodities	Two-stage stochasitic model

of specifying how many airtankers should be home-based and how much excess capacity should be used to satisfy daily airtanker deployment needs is modeled as an integer linear program with several simplifying assumptions. This model was applied regionally by Ontario Ministry of Natural Resources to place CL-215 airtankers for 1993 fire season.

An important issue in humanitarian logistics, especially in emergency services locations is the definition of objective. An analysis of private and public sector location models [130] suggests that though fundamentally the models are similar, the objectives in each sector differ. In public sector this task is harder due to the difficulty in attaching monetary value to social utility. In the 1970s extensive research was done in locating facilities on a network to reach and meet the demands of customers. Objective of these models evolved from minimizing costs to maximizing public welfare [129].

Finding "robust facility location" that will not only be well suited based on the current requirements and the state of the system, but should continue to be the best sites for the changes in the system in terms of environment, population density, and market trends may not be of immediate concern during a crisis but is relevant in the context of humanitarian logistics. Owen and Daskin [117] address the strategic nature of facility location problems by stochastic or dynamic characteristics. Dynamic treatment focuses on time perspective for longer horizon, whereas stochastic treatment focuses on uncertainty in input parameter such as demand forecast and distances. The stochastic formulations are either based on explicit probability distribution or are managed with stochasticity by scenario planning.

The location problem for the Florida County Disaster Recovery Centers is solved by modeling it as an LSCP and with a two-stage solution approach [33]. It is a great example of what can be achieved if academics, practitioners, and emergency planners collaborate in solving the problem. FEMA opens Disaster Recovery Centers (DRC) in the affected areas. The team of authors helps FEMA identify at least three (as required by FEMA) DRC sites in Alachua County, Florida, United States. Their choice of objectives is to minimize average travel distance to the closest DRC, minimize maximum travel distance to DRC, minimize total number of DRCs needed within a specified distance of a nearest DRC, and maximize probability that at least one DRC will be useable after the disaster. FEMA and the authors agreed on minimizing total number of DRCs for three different distances.

They formulate the problem as a set covering problem and solve the original model using aggregate data with Microsoft Excel by solving p-center problems in succession. It should be recognized that the authors accepted the loss of accuracy in reducing the problem size but demonstrated that the emergency planners could use the same aggregation method to simplify and increase solvability achieving user friendliness. It should be noted that this simplification does not capture the entire problem but is effective. The whole process provides a means for testing various scenarios. Various algorithms are picked for aggregation of the demand points. Important take away from this article is not just location of DRCs but some of the valuable lessons learned in such projects are that the sponsors (in this case FEMA) may not have a single overall objective, the choice of model may be subjective, data collection is most of the work, and last but not the least, simplification by aggregation of data may be necessary.

An important recommendation made by FEMA is to store critical supplies in a safe and secure location. "However, storing a set of these items at every distribution center, manufacturing facility, transportation hub, and office within the supply chain can be cost prohibitive", hence Hale and Moberg [60] propose "secure site selection process" that "can balance operational effectiveness and cost-efficiency by identifying the minimum number and possible locations of off-site storage facilities". The research combines recommendations from FEMA with LSCP model.

Using a four-step decision process the authors create a list of potential sites. The steps involved are identifying the critical resources needed at each site, identifying all critical sites within the supply chain, setting maximum response time and minimum distance goals, and using these steps to identify the numbers and approximate location of emergency resource storage facilities. Based on this candidate list an LSCP is developed to minimize the total number of sites. In addition to limiting the distances from the sites and other facilities of the humanitarian supply chain the model has constraints to incorporate the fact that the managers must "decide upon a minimum distance each secure location must be from each supply chain facility". Together, these constraints make a solution space smaller and manageable yielding solutions to this problem relatively quicker than the standard generalized network LSCP. The model finds three locations for secure sites in the three dark shaded areas from given list of seven critical facilities.

In case of a bioterrorist attack, "mass dispensing requires the rapid establishment of a network of dispensing sites and health facilities that are *flexible, scalable* and *sustainable* for medical prophylaxis and treatment of general population" [88]. Authors use facility location models to determine number of points of dispensing (POD). The model accounts for population densities, maximum travel distance, list of available private and public facilities, and the availability of staff required to operate PODs.

The approach in this research study has two steps. The first step determines the minimum number of PODs required in a given region subject to maximum distance a household has to travel. There is an additional constraint for requiring at least two PODs to incorporate the uncertainty of possible closing of one POD due to disaster. This is a capacitated FLP. This model when solved returns minimum number of PODs required. The second step minimizes average distance traveled by households for the given number of sites. In addition to sensitivity analysis offering insights into various parameters of the situation the authors compare "heterogeneous mix of PODs" such as public PODs, drive-through and walk-through PODs, private PODs for large businesses, university/college campuses, nursing homes for elderly, jails, and airport. They also point out that dispensing itself is sensitive to the availability of critical staff to operate the PODs. This research finds site locations based on diverse but necessary properties of a site. The extensive and in-depth study is then applied to mass dispensing planning effort for the Atlanta metropolitan area.

Prevention or intervention in case of disaster outbreaks may be thought of as a prepositioning strategy that is prevalent in cases such as Malaria infestation in Africa. Deploying limited resources such as facilities, labor, insecticide, and bed-nets while maximizing the reduction of risks due to Malaria with constrained budget [24] is modeled as an optimization problem and solved using heuristic. The decisions such as location of distributing centers, their covering zones, deploying of intervention in these zones, number of people protected, resources, and their allocation at distribution centers are included in the model. Rather than solving all parts simultaneously the location decision is done using heuristics whereas deployment is solved optimally. The model is applied to the case of Malaria interventions in Africa. The data are provided by WHO and all models are implemented in Excel for use by non-government organizations for countries in Africa.

Yushimito et al. [168] address the problem of facility location which can prove to be useful for prepositioning supplies in the affected area from a disaster. They formulate an uncapacitated facility location problem to minimize response time. The heuristic algorithm is based on Voronoi diagrams.

4.1.2 Logistics Planning

The research discussed so far focuses on facility location which is an integral part of preparation. However, it is extremely important to cover all aspects of planning in anticipation of disaster. Humanitarian logistics planning in case of disaster predominantly includes shipping critical supplies and services to affected areas and evacuate affected population. An overall model encompassing logistics planning in emergency situation integrating natural disaster logistics decision support system is developed by Ozdamar et al. [119]. This research, we believe, is one of the first of the kind addressing dynamic time-dependent transportation problem for ongoing aid delivery incorporating new requests for supplies and availability of modes of transportation. Though very operational in nature the model is meant for emergency planning. The authors model the situation as a hybrid of multi-commodity network flow problem and vehicle routing problem. The model can be decomposed into two multi-commodity problems, first a linear model for conventional commodities and second for vehicle flow and hence an integer model. The solution process uses Lagrangian Relaxation on arc capacity constraints. The authors test the algorithm on a small set of test instances of an earthquake scenario of realistic size.

Yi and Ozdamar [167] examine the problem of coordination of "transportation of commodities from major supply centers to distribution centers in affected areas and the transport of wounded people from affected areas to temporary and permanent emergency unit". The authors develop a mixed-integer multi-commodity network flow model treating vehicles as integer commodity flows in the first stage and providing schedules for the same using "vehicle splitting algorithm". The objective is to minimize delay in supplying critical commodities and health services. The approach is compared with vehicle routing problem single-stage formulation approach. To validate their model the authors implemented it on a possible scenario of a severe earthquake in Istanbul, Turkey using public source data.

The Center for Emergency Response Analytics (CERA) uses discrete-event simulation to evaluate POD for responding to an Anthrax attack. POD operations are deemed to be extremely complex since the "interactions among the process layout, staffing levels, physical limitations of the POD site, client transportation, and supply chain operations defy analysis by static tools and techniques, such as spreadsheets and mathematical models" [165]. Developed simulation models facilitate a complete plan for response. This model makes explicit assumptions such as restricting the attack to an island and that this was the only attack. The effectiveness of dispensing is evaluated by measuring the performance of cycle time for a family, waiting time in traffic, length of car-back-up, client population in the POD, formulation of queues in the process, and utilization of staff. The end results of the simulation identify importance of assumptions, whether community's goal was achievable, compared alternatives and more importantly evaluate how the plan would work in spite of incorrect assumptions. The simulation model is robust enough to extend to dispensing the second time around for further treatment.

"Though the location and capacities of resources provided are key components in the disaster management plan, little research has been conducted on the topic of prior planning" [126]. The authors therefore offer a two-stage stochastic optimization model for determining location and quantity of critical supplies. They model uncertainty of demand requirements and locations. They also model the uncertainties of the transportation network and loss of supplies due to disaster. The supplies include equipment, consumables, and non-consumable goods, but no services. The model is formulated with cost minimizing objective where the costs are the expected costs of supplies resulting from the supplier locations, procurement, allocation, and transportation. The model is solved and applied to southeastern United States as a case study. The case study is based on four major and four less severe hurricanes with 21 developed scenarios including isolated and combined storms with assigned probabilities of occurrence. The resulting solution specifies where storage sites should be located.

The issue of planning for transportation of critical supplies and services and deployment of emergency personnel is discussed by Barbarosoglu and Arda [11]. The authors propose a two-stage stochastic programming framework in case of an earthquake. A multi-commodity, multi-modal network is formulated to transport goods and personnel. The uncertainty of a disaster in terms of timing and severity is captured by random variables characterizing resource requirements and resource mobilization. Specifically, randomness is represented by random arc capacity, supply quantity, and demand. The two-stage stochastic programming structure of the problem has pre-event and post-event phases. The post-event phase is further divided into early response and response.

The objective function minimizes the total first-stage transportation and expected recourse cost and the constraints are standard capacity, supply, and demand constraints in addition to a recourse constraint which is determined by solving the second-stage problem for each scenario. The model is validated using data from the August 1999 earthquake in Turkey. The authors compare their computational results with wait-and-see solutions (expected value of the optimal solutions if the perfect information were available) to find value of the stochastic solution.

4.1.3 Prepositioning and Resource Allocation

Contribution by graduate military students to recent research work in humanitarian logistics has been in the area of prepositioning of resources. United States Pacific fleet operation is in the area susceptible to sudden-onset natural disasters. In addition, United States Military resources are also in danger of terroristic attacks. The humanitarian relief operations in these instances can be carried out by United States Navy due to its unique capabilities. McCall [105] identifies the need of "pre-positioned pack-up kit of first response material" for immediate deployment taking the "guesswork out of initial requirements". Two types of pack-up kits depending on hot or cold weather are prepositioned. The optimization model prescribes a candidate list of storage locations based on budget and space constraints and quality of each type of kit. The objective function minimizes the cost of delivering kits from prepositioned location to potential disaster site in the formulated location model under the assumptions that a plan for transportation and distribution is in place. The solution is found by CPLEX within an implementation of GAMS. Based on World Health Organization (WHO) Emergency Disaster Database disaster scenarios are created by varying severity and type. Sensitivity analysis performed for unlimited to limited capacities and budget provides insights.

Prepositioning in the true sense of the way should not be limited to critical supplies alone. A two-stage probabilistic model offers guidance in addition to prepositioning of critical supplies, and assets with physical, budgetary, and capacity limitations [151]. First-stage decisions describe the expansion of various assets such as warehouses, medical facilities, and airfields way before disaster strikes. In the second stage these assets are utilized to maximize "expected rescued survivors". Maximizing delivery of commodities is also part of the objective here. Second-stage decisions are based on the concept of recourse where supplies and personnel are deployed after the uncertain event of disaster has occurred and assets have already been allocated. The model is solved using GAMS and CPLEX.

This two-stage stochastic optimization model [151] is evaluated using two scenarios [62] affecting Washington D.C. metropolitan area in the United States. Viable strategic options are analyzed from a Category 4 hurricane and a one-kiloton nuclear explosion near the city center. Though notional, the approach does seem plausible since the data were gathered using public sources and subject matter experts.

The research also discusses policy issues in the United States of "gap of pain" defined as measures of time from exhaustion of local and state resources till the arrival of federal resources, which in itself was a major issue in hurricane Katrina. The study uncovers a more important humanitarian logistics question of "what, and how much do they need?" as opposed to "how much can we send?"

Salmeron and Apte [132] investigate this problem of strategic allocation of resources for humanitarian responses to future disasters further. They develop a two-stage stochastic optimization model to address key issues in current planning, focus being the pre-establishment of adequate capacity and other resources (decisions which need to be made well-in-advance before a disaster strikes), that enable efficient relief operations, with the main objective of minimizing the expected number of casualties. The research is restricted to sudden cyclical disasters which include natural events such as floods and hurricanes. The model guides the allocation of budget to acquire and position relief assets.

The study deals with uncertainty regarding the location and severity of the possible disaster by considering different scenarios, each of which may occur with a known probability. Knowing the exact scenario would be better for planning purposes, however, that would not be realistic. The model includes first-stage (strategic) decisions to represent the expansion of resources such as warehouses, medical facilities with personnel, ramp spaces, and shelters. All these decisions must be made well-in-advance of a disaster event, i.e., with only probabilistic information about its location and severity. Second-stage (operational) variables in the model plan operations spanning three days following the event. These concern the logistics of the problem, where allocated resources and contracted transportation assets are deployed to rescue and treat survivors in need of immediate medical assistance, deliver required commodities, and transport the displaced people, all of which are scenario-dependent.

Computational results on this notional test case provide insights into the problem complexity and prove the benefit of using optimization to guide budget allocation. The results show that matching existing transportation capacity and health capacity for emergency survivors appears to be the most critical issue. However, as more funding becomes available, expansion of warehouses and delivery of commodities takes priority because the cost of additional special transportation and health facilities for the last pockets of emergency survivors is too expensive. The research also assesses the benefit of the stochastic model by using "Wait-and-See" (perfect information model) and "Value of Stochastic Solution" (averaging scenarios model) analyses. It is found in their test cases the stochastic model reduces the expected number of casualties compared to deterministic models that are based on perfect information and/or average of all scenarios.

A facility location model incorporating inventory decisions developed for a sudden-onset disaster, determining the number and location of distribution centers and the quantity of inventory at each distribution center, is a variant of the maximal covering location model [10]. The objective is to maximize "the total expected demand covered by the established distribution centers". The model is applied to 286 scenarios, each defined by disaster location and its impact, and 45 candidate distribution centers are considered based on data gathered from National Geophysical Data Center. Rest of the data are hypothetical. The computational analysis shows how the "before" and "after" disaster funding affects performance of the relief system (response time and percentage of demand satisfied).

CARE International is one of the largest humanitarian organizations providing relief to the affected population of a disaster-struck area. Improving agility for acquiring resources and distributing them is critical. Collaborative research on this topic is done by CARE and Center for Humanitarian Logistics at Georgia Tech, United States. The model developed [36] evaluates the effects of prepositioning relief supplies to reduce average response time. The model tries to answer the question, "given an initial investment, what is the configuration of the network that minimizes the average response time?" The objective function in the mixed-integer program minimizes the expected average response time over demand instances. The solution offers provided guidance for CARE's managers to form the prepositioning network. The results illustrate how to best allocate existing inventory given an operating budget. The observed results do not differ significantly between the historical and simulated scenarios.

A project for CARE-USA [31] applies a global commodity tracking system to improve CARE's emergency preparedness. They propose that this will improve the inventory management and accountability through monitoring and oversight. They also improve warehousing with design and layout.

The immediate resource requirements and their temporal patterns are developed using quantitative methods by Holguin-Veras et al. [64, 65]. The researchers analyze the data set based on Action Request Forms issued after Hurricane Katrina made landfall. The data show only 150 different commodities were requested. This conclusion suggests that emergency responders should focus their efforts on transporting these commodities to reduce cycle time of delivery. In addition, regional prepositioning of these commodities will give a leg-up not only on transportation time but also will be extremely cost-effective due to reduced safety stock.

Holguin-Veras et al. [63] identify three broad categories of issues after Katrina. First, initial impact of the system through scope and scale of the needs, effects on communication system. Second, institutional issues such as lack of staff and available but untrained staff, lack of integration between systems and third, logistical issues such as inefficiencies in prepositioning, unplanned handling and distribution of donations, acquisition, and limited asset visibility.

Muckstadt et al. [112] discuss a prototype warehousing system model for response in an Anthrax attack. They propose a two-stage stochastic model to estimate the operating cost over time and the delay in emergency response for a given supply chain. The model determines inventory levels for stochasticity in timing and nature of the event. The model is optimized in both the stages when exact details are not known but the emergency event has taken place.

Most of the pandemic-related research is focused on health care issues than humanitarian logistics. However, such problems pose unique sets of challenges in emergency preparedness planning in terms of vaccine supply chain. Therefore, we offer a small sample of such articles. Araz et al. [6] study the increasing concerns about the possible social and economical disruption may arise due to such disasters. They propose a geospatial-temporal disease spread simulation model to study the effects of policies such as school closure on communities. Schindler and Radichel [139] develop an agent-based modeling setup and tool to allow real-time decision support and resource allocation for personnel of PODs conducting mass vaccination for pandemic influenza. There are numerous recent articles describing models especially using simulation.

In preparation for disasters, planning of transportation assets plays an important role. Though transportation has grown to be the second largest operating cost for humanitarian operations since 1990s [98, 99] professional fleet management is almost non-existent in smaller NGOs [98, 99, 100]. The triple-A framework [90] of agility, adaptability and alignment is used to analyze an interesting supply chain of vehicles [147, 146]. The authors in these research studies identify the objective to be agility. They achieve this by compensating with cost-effectiveness which is accomplished by sacrificing speed of the vehicles.

A research study [100] investigates the *vehicle replacement* policy in the International Committee of the Red Cross, one of the largest humanitarian organizations. They use logistic models to determine drivers of replacement and linear regression to determine the drivers of salvage value. A dynamic programming application compares costs of replacement versus status quo. Using field data collected, the models were executed and the results indicate that there will be considerable savings gain by adjusting the replacement policy.

As discussed earlier, humanitarian logistics to some extent is a response supply chain. Researchers in the following articles have treated it like one and explored various aspects of it. This focus varies from design of the supply chain to information flow in the supply chain to push–pull boundaries of the supply chain.

Resource allocation is being studied through "informal" modeling by Gralla et al. [54]. This methodology is inspired by the heuristics that humanitarian logisticians apply to design their supply chains quickly but not necessarily optimally. Johnson [73] creates an environmental sustainability scorecard for MedShare International. Surplus medical supplies and used equipment are collected by MedShare to redistribute to undeserved hospitals and clinics. The cost tradeoff includes costs from environmental impact, carbon footprint, etc. The supply chain is evaluated based on collection, facilities, shipping, and recipient. Mobile facilities are frequently used to deliver diverse and remote requests for relief. Halper and Raghavan [61] explore best strategies to route these facilities to maximize services to the affected areas.

Lack of adequate information flow results in more difficulty in managing a humanitarian supply chain. Day et al. [30] are currently working on finding issues that hinder this flow of information after a large catastrophic disaster has struck. The researcher conducted a case study by focusing on diverse sources of information including government, profit and non-profit organizations and individuals during and after the disaster. A lightweight web-based system with central database to track the available supply of beds, share the demand information, and trace the historic occupancy, is being designed and implemented by Iyer et al. [71] on a standard web browser through a simple user interface.

Islam [70] identifies potential bottlenecks in the existing business processes of the supply chain structure of a leading NGO to stay ahead of the rapidly growing operations in Africa. The conclusions lead to issues in current procurement processes, multi-levels of approval processes, inflexible policies, etc. Aviles et al. [7] address variability in the timing and quantity of donation to investigate the issue of supply chain operations. The problem modeled as a network of the WFP supply chain, decided the time and location of source and transportation of food. It is also designed to evaluate borrowing against future donations to allow for food purchases. Push pull boundaries in a drug supply chain in Zambia are being studied by Yadav [166] by exploring effects of inter-organizational coordination and risk-sharing. This drug flow supply chain coordinates amongst multiple donors. The research discusses how "push pull boundaries" can be explained using the forecast driven and order driven supplies in global health supply chain.

4.2 Disaster Response

Disaster response consists of various logistic operations as we have seen so far. In this subsection we focus on inventory management and distribution which are important part of the response supply chain. Due to the significance of these topics they have their own place in managing the supply chain issues of humanitarian logistics. However, it is important to point out that decision making is also a critical issue in disaster response and hence is discussed in this subsection.

4.2.1 Inventory Management

As every researcher in the field of operations management and operations research knows extensive research has been (and is being) done on the topic of Inventory Management, and a large number of research articles have been written on the topic. However, a literature survey revealed that very few studies have dealt directly with the management of inventory in humanitarian relief or disaster response. In dealing with a disaster, due to unreliability of transportation infrastructure, inventory management becomes all the more critical and hence this topic needs attention from researchers. We believe, the body of research carried out without the emergency context can be adapted, to some extent, for managing inventory in humanitarian operations in areas such as warehousing of critical supplies, determining inventory levels in distribution centers, and stockpiling prophylaxis in case of bioterrorism or a pandemic. Summary of some of the articles reviewed in inventory management is given in Table 4.2.

The unpredictable consequences of the disasters, and due to unknown characteristics, their uncertain remedies give rise to irregular supply and demand patterns. In addition, there exist issues that are inherent in disaster situations which "surpass the capabilities of current

Table 4.2. Summary of literature review on inventory management.

Article	Major decision	Objective	Method
Beamon and Kotleba [15]	Optimal order quantities and reorder points for long-term emergency relief response	Optimize inventory management	Stochastic inventory control model
Bravata et al. [21]	Stockpile of prophylaxis and dispensing	Evaluate costs and benefits of alternative strategies for inventory of prophylaxis	Supply chain model based on four strategies
Lodree and Taskin [95]	Proactive disaster recovery planning	Optimize inventory management	Stochastic inventory control model formulated with Bayesian updates

emergency approaches" [16]. The authors address one of the limitations of the current literature on inventory management in humanitarian logistics by "developing a stochastic inventory control model that determines optimal order quantities and reorder points for a long term emergency relief response".

The authors develop this model for responding to crisis in Sudan. The multi-supplier inventory model develops an inventory policy taking into consideration the unique demand patterns over a long-term complex humanitarian relief response. Their models are extensions of continuous review inventory models with two options for resupply [110]. Beamon and Kotleba [16] develop this model using two reorder levels (r_1 and r_2) and two-order quantities (Q_1 and Q_2) one for normal supplies and the other for emergency supplies. They assume $r_1 > r_2$ and lead time τ_1 of the first order to be greater than τ_2, the lead time of the emergency reorder. The model gives higher fixed and per unit ordering costs to emergency reorders than the first order. The authors assume that international supplier does not run out of supplies, an order quantity is large enough to cover the first reorder so as not to trigger an additional reorder ($Q_1 > r_1$), second lead time for emergency orders and demand occurring is discrete 10-day interval. In addition, for simplification, they assume replenishment lead time for normal orders to be constant. The model is solved using five-step procedure. Data for the implementation were collected on-site at Lockichoggio, Kenya. The research is one of the earlier strategic steps in developing inventory levels for humanitarian relief.

An application of three single-item inventory management strategies to humanitarian relief operations in South Sudan [15] "demonstrates the performance benefits of using quantitative methods to manage inventory in a relief setting". First strategy is based on the model discussed above [16], second is a "heuristic humanitarian relief model" using simulation. This approach identifies factors critical to the performance of the system and also confirms that it was adaptable and could be easily modified to incorporate changes, strategic or operational. This model demonstrates consequences of backorders. Third strategy based on the "naive" model was simplistic but was not as effective as the other two.

In most circumstances, a relief worker is not in a position to compute optimal solutions due to lack of technology and time [15, 155]. In addition, due to high turnover of staff, volunteer participation and limited funding, inventory management policies need to be "easy to implement, flexible to change and require little effort to maintain". Therefore, a heuristic may be more suitable in such circumstances than an exact algorithm. The heuristics proposed in the second strategy, called "Silver-Meal heuristic" [141], selects replenishment quantity so that the total cost per unit time for the duration of replenishment is minimized. The approach used in this heuristics does not guarantee a global optimal but guarantees a local minimum for holding and set-up costs. Based on the implementation and analysis, this strategy with a lower cost accomplishes greater flexibility. The drawback of this strategy is that under certain scenario it reorders large quantities making storage difficult especially in the relief period.

Following articles explore interesting aspects of inventory management such as non-traditional models, assumptions that demand is a function of hurricane characteristics and tradeoffs between modes of transportation. One of the fundamental issues for humanitarian logisticians responding to bioterrorism is the inventory of prophylaxis. It is therefore important to analyze the strategies that will maintain and dispense local and regional supplies of antibiotics and medical items [21]. The authors do not use a mathematical model but the situation is modeled by considering the local and regional supply chain as well as local capacity based on four strategies. The strategies are, enhance bioterrorism event detection, increase local dispensing capacity, increase local inventories, and increase deployed inventory. The authors conclude that mortality is highly dependent on the local dispensing capacity, the number of individuals requiring prophylaxis, adherence to prophylactic antibiotics, and delays in attack detection. If regional inventories can be made available, the bottleneck is local dispensing capacity. Hence it is more beneficial to increase such dispensing capacity rather than to increase inventory.

McCoy [108] develops an inventory management model for investigating two tradeoffs, expensive airlift of a product for speedy delivery versus less expensive but slower shipment (and thus the ability to ship more total material), and acquisition and management of an expensive stockpile versus more budget allocated to quick response. A mathematical approach to Triage is being developed by Uzun et al. [163] to identify effective dynamic triage rules to maximize total lives saved.

In case of natural disasters such as hurricanes, the prepositioning of assets and inventory levels at warehouses is complicated due to the uncertainty in the number of hurricanes expected to make landfall. The humanitarian relief organizations rely on pre-contracted vendors and retailers for critical supplies like batteries, flashlights, generators, etc. Therefore, it is important to analyze the problem from the perspective of manufacturers or retailers [95]. The statistical model is formulated "as an optimal stopping problem with Bayesian updates, where updates are based on hurricane predictions". The authors assume that hurricane-related demand is a function of hurricane characteristics such as its intensity and path, and they further assume that demand is a function of storm's maximum sustained wind speed. The model considers demands associated with "regular" hurricane as well as "extreme" hurricane. The distribution for random variable that specifies whether the storm is extreme is Bernoulli. The order (or production cost) is an increasing sequence for forecast updates. The approach is based on the concept from emergency management that "risk identification is an integral part of the planning process". The model is implemented for data from HURDAT database, which is a database maintained by the National Hurricane Center of attributes of hurricanes since 1851 in the Atlantic Basin.

A comprehensive data is analyzed to confirm a common belief that in an economic downturn food banks face difficulties to serve the needy [57]. Of interest here is the way inventory is evaluated, not by weight but by nutritional value. The researchers develop a model for one-commodity pick up and delivery vehicle routing problem and employ various methods to solve the problem.

4.2.2 Distribution

In a disaster response or humanitarian relief mission the emergency planners encounter problems of transporting critical supplies from the

50 *Supply Chain Issues in Humanitarian Logistics*

Table 4.3. Summary of literature review on distribution.

Article	Major decision	Objective	Method
Ekici et al. [39]	Food distribution logistics during pandemic and intervention strategies	Maximize distribution of food to victims of pandemic	Disease spread model integrated with facility location and resource allocation
Ergun et al. [43]	Choose facilities	Minimize travel time and facility congestion	Network model with congestion games using Nash equilibrium for polynomial time
Feng and Keller [46]	Qualitatively and quantitatively evaluate distribution plans	Establish distribution plan that satisfies both local and national governments objectives	Multiple-objective decision analysis
Khan and Richter [75]	Determine alternate modes of dispensing in Dept. of Health, Los Angeles County	Optimize dispensing of prophylaxis	Multi-criterian decision analysis
Lee et al. [86, 87]	Plan large-scale emergency dispensing	Minimize total cost in terms of cycle time, throughput, and actual cost at POD	Resource allocation model and simulation
Liang et al. [94]	Analyze error disaster avoidance mechanism	Improve information distribution reliability	Fault-tolerant system design with several layers of hierarchical setup

source to the affected areas within a given time frame. Though this can be handled as a prepositioning strategy, the problem can also be modeled as a distribution problem. Some of the research articles in distribution are summarized in Table 4.3.

Rathi et al. [125] formulate the problem of distribution with three linear programming formulations. First two formulations minimize the tardiness of supplies delivered within the specified time window. The models do this by determining which transportation assets can be optimally allocated in each time period. The third model distributes the lateness evenly over all routes. The formulation of this type offers "tradeoffs between the degree of control to be exercised by the planner

4.2 Disaster Response

and the speed of computation". The models were implemented at United States Transportation Command within the Deployment Analysis Prototype System.

Emergency planners work together with the Center for Disease Control (CDC) for a response to bioterrorism or pandemic by means of planning mass dispensing of prophylaxis. In addition to locating the right POD at right place, Lee et al. [86, 87] develop a decision support system. The system combines optimization tools with simulation techniques. The relative fast execution of the system shows that "a real-time decision support system is viable through careful design of a stand-alone simulator coupled with powerful tailor-designed optimization solvers". This extensive study brings flexibility to "what if" scenarios of the decision support system. The distribution of medications can be conveniently altered proving it to be an invaluable tool, not only in mass dispensing, but in training the planners and strategically preparing for disaster response. The speed and the flexibility also contribute to "dynamic on-the-fly reconfiguration of large PODs."

The authors [86, 87] point out that though there do exist similarities between POD network and manufacturing and service system design there also are some fundamental differences such as estimates of parameters and distribution due to uncertainty of human behavior during receiving or dispensing of medication in a disaster situation. The POD site is modeled as an open queuing network where the nodes of a directed graph represent stations in the process. The staffing problem is modeled as an optimization problem. The objective is to minimize the total cost, measured in terms of cycle time, throughput, and cost at each station. This is subject to, in addition to integrality constraints, number of workers allocated to each station being within an interval and availability of workers. The model developed is a mixed-integer program with non-linear objective function. Simulation assists the optimization in resolving and updating the resource allocation statistics. The system was validated as a field study with 864,000 households by replicating the smallpox tests performed by [103].

One of the effective safety measures common to thyroid cancer, resulting from exposure to radioactive iodine in a nuclear incident, is potassium iodide (KI). Hence, the distribution plans for KI are necessary in preparing for such disasters [46]. The authors develop a multiple-objective decision analysis tool to "qualitatively and quantitatively" evaluate the plans for a hypothetical region. The decision makers in such situations, government agencies both nationwide and local, must be in agreement about the objective. A hierarchy of objectives can help them make a better decision. The multiple objectives are converted to single-attribute value function by adding the values with swing weights to solve the problem. The "what if" analysis is made possible by choosing different weights for different regions ("sliders").

Research study by Sheu [140] presents a hybrid fuzzy clustering-optimization approach to the distribution of critical supplies in the affected areas during the rescue period. Based on five assumptions related to the affected areas and their geographic location — the supply sources, relief distribution centers and channels, disaster-induced damage conditions and casualties, time varying relief demand, and types of relief supplies — the model is developed using the following steps: time-varying relief demand forecast, grouping of the affected areas (this involves binary transformation for fuzzy clustering), determination of distribution priority, group-based relief distribution, and finally, dynamic relief supply. The research validates the approach based on the massive earthquake in Taiwan in September 1999. The numerical results reported show that the performance can be improved to 30.6% using this approach.

Last mile distribution is hard enough in commercial supply chain but due to the unique challenges it is even harder in disaster response and in humanitarian relief. Reaching the affected areas from local distribution centers (LDCs) is discussed by Balcik et al. [10] by developing an optimization model. The principal decisions are allocation of critical supplies to LDCs and delivery scheduling of vehicles. Demand is divided in to two groups, Type 1 and Type 2. Type 1 demand (tools, blankets, etc.) occurs once at the start of the planning horizon. Type 2 demand consists of consumable goods occurs periodically. The first type is large in quantity whereas the second type may not be so and for this no backorders exist. The mixed-integer programming model minimizes the sum of routing and penalty costs. The approach has two phases. In the first phase all possible delivery routes are generated. A candidate list is extracted from these routes by preprocessing for consideration the infrastructure changes or the availability of vehicles. Based on the list of routes, periods to visit each demand location, the amount of supplies and type, and the delivery routes are identified by executing the model in the second phase. The authors validate this approach by implementing the model using numerical examples. The example helps illustrate relationship between decision variables and parameters. Solution times are long for larger problems.

Distribution of critical supplies may be accomplished if the affected population can reach the supplies as opposed to supplies reaching the individuals. These individuals are "decentralized decision makers who choose to visit one of a number of facilities opened by a centralized planner" [43]. Choice of the facility to visit depends on the individual and that behavior impacts the system of self-help. Instances of such distribution may be during a pandemic or a slow-onset disaster.

The model being developed in this research can have two objectives, one standard objective of minimizing the travel time and the other, more expanded version that includes facility congestion. Due to this objective the problem becomes asymmetric network configuration game. The network is defined with costs on arcs as delays experienced by the users. The flow on the network is "unweighted, unsplittable, and atomic". The model examines the problem of mutual assignment with individuals wanting to minimize their own cost and the centralized planner trying to minimize the system-wide cost. Equilibrium solution for the first objective is found easily with tight bounds on the prices of "anarchy and stability". Nash equilibrium for the second objective is found in polynomial time. The authors conclude that using only optimization approach leads to poor system performance for decentralized decision making. Therefore, they integrate that approach with game theory to develop these models.

Lessons learned from past incidents of pandemic cases suggest that efficient and quick response can reduce morbidity, mortality, and costs to the community. In collaboration with American Red Cross, Ekici et al. [39] develop a "disease spread model" integrating facility location and resource allocation network model for food distribution. They also develop a heuristics to find "near-optimal solutions in large instances". First an individual-based continuous time stochastic model for influenza transmission is constructed comprising the progress of the disease within an infected person and the spread amongst the affected population with extension in the form of intervention such as voluntary quarantine or school closure. Then they develop a "capacitated multi-period hierarchical facility location problem (CMPH-FLP)". Since this is an NP-hard problem, which is difficult to solve with a commercial solvers, an "Add-Drop" heuristic is also developed. Using these models and solution approach they propose resolution for location of major facilities and PODs, closing of these sites based on need for food and minimum cost to serve target population by allocating food. For the food distribution network a deterministic as well as dynamic approach was compared with "Perfect Solution" benchmark case. Authors report that deterministic models could be used in advance planning whereas dynamic models are more appropriate for response. The approach was validated by implementing the models in the state of Georgia.

Another research study for choosing modes of dispensing prophylaxis based on multi-criterion decision analysis is done and implemented in Los Angeles County by Khan and Richter [74, 75]. The authors follow six steps, identifying stakeholders, deciding on objective hierarchy based on relevant measures, identifying value functions, identifying weight of relative importance, assessing the alternatives, and conducting sensitive analysis in the context of mass dispensing of prophylaxis. This research study including the model (especially the transportation model) and analyses helped the Department of Health at Los Angeles County to gain support from their plan in alternative modes of dispensing. It also provided insight for the emergency planners. The authors point out however, that "the process can be repeated by any jurisdiction but definition of "best" will rely on issues and gaps that are identified with the jurisdiction's POD plans for mass prophylaxis.

Apte and Ferrer [4] identify the essential infrastructure needed to develop a cold-chain distribution network for vaccine in a military application. They develop a network distribution model for transportation of elements needed for successful vaccine flow through the network. Various characteristics of the supply chain are identified, including a discussion on metrics of distribution centers, support for these and the inventory necessary at these centers. In addition, they follow the information and vaccine flow through the distribution network.

Griffin [55] studies efficiencies and effectiveness of drug distribution in Zambia. The study first follows forecasting and then creates map of transportation. The researcher proposes changes to supply chain structure and distribution strategies. Since the current system fails due to duplication, costs overrun, inadequate supply, and uncertainties of donations. Menezes and Varela [109] analyze real requirement of medical and non-food items for Medicos Sin Fronteras. They also investigate optimal distribution policies by comparing air and/or sea routes. The researchers use Zimbabwe for case study.

Distribution of blood by monitoring collection and usage patterns is being studied with validation through a case study in Zambia by Osuntogun et al. [116]. The forecasting model is based on probabilistic model of individual units of blood. Flow assignment of blood from collection centers to transfusion outlets with fair and efficient utilization of resources.

Distribution of vaccines and prophylaxis in the event of a substantial public health emergency is a necessity that requires planning on part of state or local health departments. King and Muckstadt [76] create numerous mathematical models focusing on the entire response network of strategic national stockpile of Center for Disease Control. Some of the logistics questions they pose and develop the models for are about the location of warehouses [112], policies of locating the facilities and their effects on costs and resource requirements, optimal levels of inventory under unbounded capacity to balance inventory costs and backorder penalties, capacities of all the resources in the response supply chain such as staff at PODs, optimal levels of service, and allocation of additional investment for improving services.

In addition to actual distribution of critical physical supplies and medical services, there exist some other important factors in distribution. For instance, it is also essential that individuals receive the updated contents of the software when accessed. A research study [94] "analyzes the error situations of a proposed content-delivering service that has been implemented in a large-scaled company in Taiwan". Disasters can cause computers to crash and thus interrupt transmission of data which results in hindering of emergency information distribution. The authors propose "disaster avoidance mechanism" based on reliability model and waiting-time distribution of disconnectivity. They describe a fault-tolerant design of the system which they then implement within a large service company with several layers in a hierarchical setup. The study claims that such an approach, though very expensive, is "clearly" more reliable than a six-sigma continuous improvement process.

The delivery of critical supplies and services to the affected area gives rise to a convergence process since personnel, information, and material flow toward the affected area. Holguin-Veras and Destro [63] focus on quantifying this material convergence by assembling a database derived from Katrina donations. They investigate whether donations can be explained in terms of the severity of the disaster or by socioeconomic properties of the geographical location of the event and donors. Such research can help in the management of donations in the response process.

4.2.3 Decision Making

Decision making in case of an emergency, whether natural or manmade, is difficult due to various uncertainties and the lack of information. Yet it must be carried out quickly and correctly. Developing decision support systems is a fundamental aspect of humanitarian logistics. Some of the articles in decision making are summarized in Table 4.4.

Dai et al. [28] study design and development of "emergency decision support systems (EDSS)". They compare the "conventional decision making (CDM)" with "emergency decision making (EDM)". They develop a computerized safety protection and disaster response for coal mines in China. The models discussed are "ventilation network model, escape evacuation model and rescue materials demand model". The ventilation network model takes into account a set of non-linear algebraic equations incorporating various environmental issues. The escape evacuation model is a multichannel quickest path problem with weighted network. And rescue materials problem are a set of "experience formulas". The authors report that using a distributed system

4.2 Disaster Response

Table 4.4. Summary of literature on decision making.

Article	Major decision	Objective	Method
Ak et al. [1]	Demand forecasting, transportation cost estimation, bid award allocation	Minimize costs and maximize service to recipients	Forecasting, transportation cost estimation and bid award allocation models
Dai et al. [28]	Design and development of computerized support systems for emergency decision making	Compare conventional decision making with emergency decision making	Non-linear algebraic equations and multichannel quickest path model with weighted network.
Engineer et al. [42]	Disease prevention/ immunizing vaccination schedule for children	Optimize vaccination schedules for childhood immunization	Dynamic programming
Regnier and Harr [128]	Evaluate trade-off between lead time and forecast accuracy	Minimize cost (or fatalities)	Discrete Markov chain model

helps users share data, models, and knowledge, but more importantly they are able to utilize subject matter experts.

In anticipation of a disaster, humanitarian relief or disaster response is predominantly posed as a cost (or fatalities) minimizing problem sometimes using stochasticity for location and severity. However, "the value of waiting for updated forecasts" is "neglected" [128]. The authors develop a decision model where the decision maker expects and plans for updated forecasts. The accuracy of forecast increases as lead time for preparation decreases. They model the situation as a discrete Markov chain. The value derived from expected forecasts depends on the "specific alternatives and cost profile" of the decision maker. An implementation to areas such as Norfolk, Virginia and Galveston, Texas, in the United States show a conceptual saving of up to 8% when compared to iterative static solutions.

Decision making in Public Health and Medicine is increasingly made based on mathematical and simulation models in case of disaster response. Brandeau et al. [20] review these models and offer recommendation for best practices for developing such model. This is a survey of all such models and a position paper. The authors propose that the response model address real-world problems, be user friendly, cover complex issues in a simple manner, include relevant outcomes, and incorporate uncertainties. The authors conclude that such models are critical for effective planning for responding to disaster, especially in the health sector and their recommendation "can increase the applicability and interpretability of future models, thereby improving strategic, tactical and operational aspects of preparedness planning and response" [20].

The World Health Organization (WHO), through the Pan American Health Organization (PAHO), acquires vaccines for 37 countries in Latin America and the Caribbean [1]. Currently a team of researchers from PAHO and Georgia Tech are developing an analytical tool kit to make decisions about demand forecasting, transportation costs, and bid awards in order to improve the supply chain for vaccines.

Carbajal et al. [23] are conducting research to understand which analytical methodology leads to better decisions in Debris Management.

4.3 Relief Operations

Relief operations belong at the end of the response supply chain in continuation of providing relief. These constitute on transportation of critical supplies and evacuation of the affected. Both of these rely heavily on robustness of the infrastructure. However, a menace to both these issues is disruption of traffic.

4.3.1 Transportation

As mentioned in the earlier subsection, Rathi et al. [125], offered three models for distribution as well as transportation of critical supplies for carrying out the relief operations within given time windows. Haghani and Oh [58] develop a large-scale multi-commodity, multi-modal network flow problem with time windows to transport a variety of critical supplies using a vehicle fleet from sources to affected areas in time, effectively and efficiently. The model can be an important part of decision-making tool for emergency planner. They convert a physical network to time–space network to incorporate the dynamic decision process. The traffic on the physical network is divided into three types. First (routing) type of traffic moves on from one node to another node on a certain type of vehicle, second (transfer) type of traffic changes mode of transportation at a node and the third type carries the supply or demand over to the next time period. The assumptions are that transfer is allowed at transshipment nodes which include origin nodes that are also transshipment nodes and all costs are linear. The objective function minimizes the sum of "the vehicular flow costs, the commodity flow costs, the supply or demand carry-over costs and transfer costs over all time periods". The three sets of constraints, include commodity flow constraints, vehicular flow constraints, and linkage constraints between vehicles and commodity flow.

The authors report two solution approaches, one decomposes the model into sub-problems by relaxing linkage constraints and the other fixes integer variables, at every iteration. They implement the model on artificially generated data set on a "medium-sized physical network". The empirical study designed to analyze robustness suggests that the model is sensitive to the arc capacity, vehicle capacity, vehicular flow costs and demand carry-over costs, moderately sensitive in certain range of demand and supply, and very sensitive beyond that. It is also moderately sensitive to commodity flow costs and supply carry-over costs and insensitive to transfer costs.

In a disaster situation, especially earthquake and flooding, when roads are not traversable, helicopter missions are common. The emergency personnel or decision makers need an efficient and effective procedure to deploy the suitable crew/fleet configuration or appropriate flight routes. Barbarosoglu et al. [12] develop mathematical models for such situations. The models execute the operational and tactical missions of,

"D1: the determination of the helicopter fleet composition by assigning helicopters from the air force bases to the operation base.

D2: the assignment of pilots with given aviation capabilities to the helicopters.

D3: the determination of the number of tours to be undertaken by each helicopter.
D4: the vehicle routing of helicopters from the operation base to disaster points in the emergency area.
D5: the load/unload, delivery, transshipment and rescue plans of each helicopter in every tour.
D6: the re-fueling schedule of each helicopter at the operation base."

The decomposed model at the top level makes a decision on D1, D2, and D3 whereas at the base level it makes a decision on D4, D5, and D6. The objective in the first case minimizes the cost of selecting different helicopters and pilots from the air force bases whereas at the base level it minimizes maximum tour duration among all helicopter which include refueling times. The solution approach is an iterative process that exchanges information between the tactical problem and operational problem which the authors call "Hierarchical multi-criteria approach". The approach is implemented on databased on scenarios similar to disaster relief data from the Turkish Army. The scenarios are kept dimensionally small due to computational complexity of the problem. The contribution of the study lies in the result that a decision maker, based on his preference and aspirations can choose from "non-dominated" solutions.

DeAngelis et al. [32] incorporate the travel of airplanes between depots and destinations and parking of the airplane during the nights for World Food Program (WFP) in Angola. The problem can be described by depots (each one with limited supply and parking space), planes having the same capacity for carrying supplies but having varying speed (can park at any depot subject to availability) and communities where food is being delivered (food measured in plane-load and time measured in days). The depots are identified in five types based on where a plane parks the previous day and present day. The objective function maximizes the total satisfied demand subject to supply–demand constraints, and fairly standard vehicle routing constraints. One fundamental constraint that is included is based on classification of depots. Effectiveness of the model is checked using four test cases based on WFP Angola records for May 2001. The implementation improved number of trips by 9–23%. The authors believe that the weekly schedules produced by the model are a good starting point for decision makers.

Table 4.5 summarizing research done so far in transportation.

Table 4.5. Summary of literature on transportation.

Article	Major decision	Objective	Method
Balcik et al. [10]	Allocate relief supplies at local distribution centers and determine delivery schedule/routes	Minimize transportation cost and maximize the benefits to recipients	Mixed-integer programming model
Barbarosoglu et al. [12]	Determine number of helicopters, number of tours, their routing and delivery schedules	Minimize cost of selecting helicopters/pilots and maximum tour duration among all helicopters	Hierarchical multi-criteria and two-level decomposition
Barbarosoglu and Arda [11]	Transportation of critical supplies and services	Minimize transportation and recourse cost	Two-stage stochastic model; multi-commodity, multi-modal network
DeAngelis et al. [32]	Plan for travel between depots and clients, deliver and park at depot	Maximize total satisfied demand	Integer linear programming model
Eksioglu et al. [40]	Determine routes for vehicles without communication means in a disaster	Maximize system mobility	Optimization and simulation models
Haghani and Oh [58]	Transportation of supplies and relief personnel	Minimize sum of vehicular flow costs, commodity flow costs, the supply or demand carry-over costs, and transfer costs	Large-scale multi-commodity, multi-modal network
Sheu [140]	Distribution of relief supplies	Optimize distribution of critical supplies in affected areas	Hybrid fuzzy clustering-optimization

4.3.2 Evacuation

As mentioned earlier, evacuation is a significant part of relief operations. In disaster situations government and non-government officials arrange to evacuate people with or without their own transportation. This type of evacuation involves various issues. Type of disaster will dictate total or partial evacuation to distant or near-by relief location and whether it is long term or temporary. Condition of the infrastructure will force which mode of transport to use but the evacuation also depends on the available fleet of vehicles and their capacity. Circumstances surrounding the evacuee, whether they are able or not, physically, financially, or emotionally also play major roles. Summary of some of the research in evacuation in Table 4.6 is given.

Table 4.6. Summary of literature on evacuation.

Article	Major decision	Objective	Method
Bakuli and Smith [8]	Resize passageways	Improve throughput and total egress time	Queuing network model
Chiu and Zheng [25]	Simultaneous mobilization destination, traffic assignment, and departure schedule	Minimize travel time over entire system	Linear programming model
Regnier [127]	Reduced decision lead times from 72 to 48 hours	Relationship between decision making lead time and Atlantic hurricane uncertainty	Stochastic model of storm movement and statistical hurricane track model
Regnier and Harr [128]	Evacuation	Explore relationship between lead time and track uncertainty	Simulation and analysis
Sayyady and Eksioglu [138]	Evacuating affected population dependent on public transit	Minimize number of casualties and total evac time	Mixed-integer linear program and Tabu search algorithm
Yi and Ozdamar [167]	Logistics planning for dispatching commodities and evacuation of wounded	Minimize unsatisfied demand and waiting of the wounded (service delay)	Mixed-integer, multi-commodity network flow model

One of the major decisions in evacuation in case of a disaster is the confinement of the structure from which one needs to evacuate. Bakuli and Smith [8] investigate the problem of designing emergency evacuation networks by extending the state-dependent queuing network models by incorporating the mean value analysis algorithm within Powell's derivative free constrained optimization algorithm. They discuss the effect of change in circulation widths on throughput and implement the design to resize passageways which in turn improve "both throughput and total egress time".

A more focused issue of evacuating "multi-priority groups (MPG)" is studied by Chiu and Zheng [25]. For suddenonset disasters they develop a Linear Programming model for multiple emergency responses and evacuation of MPG to different destinations with varying priority. The authors assume that guidance for evacuation is done ideally, the population of evacuees is known, the area from which evacuation is to take place is known, and the "complete evacuation scenario is of interest and there is no shadow evacuation". Under these assumptions the objective is to minimize travel time over the entire system based on priorities. The problem is then transformed from algebraic formulation to Matrix form for facilitation of obtaining solution in a user-friendly platform. The approach was validated on a test network of 8 nodes and 14 directed arcs. The authors believe that this study is a starting point for "modeling a complex evacuation logistics mobilization problem".

In addition to actual evacuation, a major issue in a disaster (especially hurricane) response for evacuation decisions is that the forecasts provide imperfect information. A research study [127] uses a stochastic model of movement of storm to explore relationship between the lead time for decision making and uncertainty of tracking the Atlantic hurricanes. A statistical hurricane track model [128] is used for strike probabilities. The author reports the results of this relationship as reducing decision lead times from 72 hours to 48 hours could reduce evacuation costs. The article also examines the cost of false alarms.

Emergency planners frequently depend on public transit system for evacuation in the case of a suddenonset disaster, especially in the urban areas. Sayyady and Eksioglu [138] propose a methodology that would be beneficial for evacuating affected population that depends on public transit for mobility. The proposed model is a mixed-integer linear programming problem where the objective function minimizes the number of casualties and total evacuation time. The prototype problem is solved using Tabu search algorithm on a numerical example with generated data. To validate the approach authors implemented it to the south-central part of the city of Fort Worth, Texas, United States. They also conduct simulation study to examine the quality of solutions obtained by Tabu search.

During Hurricane Katrina in United States the evacuation plan required the affected people to meet up with buses at select locations in order to be evacuated. Unfortunately, this type of plan does not help those people who are unable to move themselves to the designated meeting locations. Post-Katrina Emergency Management Reform Act in the United States of 2006 states that state or local governments have the responsibility to coordinate evacuation plans for all populations, including those with disabilities. Apte and Heath [5] develop an optimization model to build an executable routing in order to dispatch multiple vehicles to pick up disabled persons from their individual locations and evacuate them. They plan to test the model by identifying a geographic location, and testing the model with sample data.

A research study [40] incorporates an information center that uses prediction and optimization models and heuristic algorithms to generate alternate routes due to disruption in traffic and infrastructure that are results of a disaster. The proposed framework was tested using simulation model on a generated scenario. The results show that the proposed framework increases the mobility and average speed.

Minimizing the effects of disruption in traffic flow due to disasters, natural or manmade, is critical for various reasons. Jin and Eksioglu [72] develop a mathematical model to reduce the delay by incorporating a prediction model for vehicles without communication capabilities or for vehicles that use a communication tool called QUALCOM. An algorithm is also proposed to update the parameters of the mathematical model. The model and the algorithm are being tested using simulated disaster scenario. The results so far suggest that the proposed models improve mobility and average speed.

In this section, we discussed the factors that influence the effectiveness and efficiency of humanitarian supply chain, such as prepositioning and facility location, inventory management, distribution, transportation, evacuation, and decision making, in view of preparation, response, and relief. However, in addition to the operational issues organizational issues are also critical. The focus of the next section is on organizational factors that affect humanitarian logistics.

5

Organizational Issues in Humanitarian Logistics

The organizational issues that will facilitate humanitarian logistics include several factors that are strategic. We focus on some of the issues listed as follows:

- Collaboration among players
- Training and education of emergency staff
- Role of donors and their donations
- Information and knowledge management
- Risk management.

The order here does not necessarily indicate the relative importance of the factors. For example, according to Tomasini and Van Wassenhove [158] information and knowledge management are two most critical issues whereas approaching humanitarian logistics from risk management perspective [77, 85, 158] is considered important for assessing disruption to supply chains [9, 17, 47, 48, 50, 51, 91, 89, 131, 145].

5.1 Collaboration

Humanitarian organizations offer stability during disaster through relief operations. Gibbons [53] raises questions about collaboration among emergency planners, community leaders, and non-profit agencies through organizational issues. The author identifies attributes of disaster response that may increase effectiveness of operation. Collaboration also needs to happen at all level [121]. Especially, the population affected by the disaster must be a part of the solution for relief and be engaged in the recovery effort.

Examining the past experience reveals the critical need for collaboration and coordination [158] among not only the humanitarian organizations but also among the military, private and humanitarian sectors [124, 134, 164]. One of the primary collaboration, especially for transportation and distribution of critical supplies and services and security of these activities, is between military and humanitarian agencies. "The use of military forces in emergency relief can offer benefits to the international relief system, although such involvement is controversial due to a number of practical, political and ethical issues" [124]. Although military is strong in logistical and organizational structure, due to its primary goal is fighting the wars, this goal is perceived to be in somewhat of a conflict with the goal of humanitarian assistance.

Having said the above, there have been numerous instances, including during Hurricane Katrina, where division of United States Marine Corps (USMC), "Combat Logistics Battalion (CLB) for Marine Expeditionary Unit has the inherent mission of providing initial support to humanitarian assistance (HA) operations" [149]. Military assets provide unique capabilities not found in the civilian humanitarian response system [101]. United Nations Office of Coordination of Humanitarian Affairs (OCHA) believes that proximity and understanding of the neighboring countries' political, social, and geographic environment is the reason why military assets are usually the first ones to be deployed. However, there remain challenges in this civil–military collaboration in terms of principles versus pragmatism and lack of military doctrine and training in humanitarian relief operations.

Collaboration between public (humanitarian) agencies and private sector is also a necessity in humanitarian supply chain, especially in the last mile distribution [157]. However, due to their inherently opposing characteristics, whereby humanitarian organizations can be slow and bureaucratic while "the other a fast-moving action-oriented business", collaboration can become difficult [164]. Yadav [166] describes how collaboration amongst multiple donors can improve the global supply chain for medicines. Such examples illustrate the need and the type of collaboration and the success of the same among various players. It should be noted that such collaboration critically depends on sharing information and taking actions based on lessons learned.

Building relationships is critical in humanitarian logistics. Eggenhofer et al. [37] explore design options for crisis response management and its information and communication technology. Sotnikov [144] studies effects of partnerships of local health departments on preparedness in case of a disaster. Statistical significance between the correlations quantifies the findings.

5.2 Information and Knowledge Management

Information Management is critical to the success or failure of humanitarian logistics [101]. In addition, as discussed earlier, a humanitarian supply chain needs to be agile. It can only achieve agility through an effective information infrastructure and knowledge of requirements in the affected area [90, 115, 158]. A humanitarian supply chain can gauge and respond to the demand, if, the gathering of information does not pose a formidable challenge. As was found in the first two earthquakes in El Salvador in 2001 the information assessment of "what was affected, what was needed, what resources were available, and as the aid began to arrive spontaneously, what was coming and when" was necessary for responding quickly [159]. Information may become available in phases and hence it needs to be managed accordingly — first, when the event happens; second, when requirements of the affected areas are known; third, when deployment begins and what is sent is known; and fourth, when it is determined whether the right kind of supplies and services have been deployed. A well-managed information system in a humanitarian supply chain is characterized by having visibility, transparency, and accountability [158]. Visibility into the flow of supplies and services, transparency of the process of transportation and distribution that can identify issues in efficiency, and accountability of the players within the supply chain, form three pillars of information management.

Every time a disaster strikes, lessons are learned by all involved. A humanitarian organization collaborates and coordinates during that disaster and in addition to field experience it also learns about the cultures of all the players involved including the affected population. As Tomasini and Van Wassenhove [158] point out, knowledge is created and is needed at different levels. In the affected areas the knowledge resides with the people, at the supply chain level it resides in the process, and it also resides at the contextual level. Untrained staff and turnover among emergency planners and responders (due to high level of stress) mandate that knowledge management must belong at the core of a humanitarian supply chain.

One of the lessons learned from Hurricane Katrina is that people with chronic illness or disabilities face unique and significant challenges. Kulemeka [84] is studying to examine how U. S. and Canadian cities are using the web to inform how to manage such challenges especially during disaster.

5.3 Training and Education

There exists a general consensus that untrained or uneducated personnel may hinder the efficiency and effectiveness of humanitarian logistics. One of the five fundamental keys to being prepared is human resources [158]. Humanitarian organizations often face the problem of inadequate staffing due to various reasons such as high turnover and requirement of diverse skill-set. Moreover, frequently this staff is neither well-trained nor well selected (especially when it comes to volunteer staff). But this pool of personnel must be adequately trained and educated in various aspects of humanitarian logistics due to the unique set of activities and environment they must operate in. This points to the need of standardization of training in emergency planning and field operations. The establishment of such standards would "help ensure comparability, quality assurance and international compatibility of training" [2].

5.4 Role of Donors and Donations

The main difficulty with donors is that they are suppliers as well as customers. They are suppliers since they donate the commodities or monies for the commodities. But at the same time they only donate with generosity provided they are convinced that donations are reaching the needy. As a party interested in assessing performance they are also customers of this supply chain. In addition, it is difficult to forecast the type and quantity of donations that may become available. There is high uncertainty about what is going to be provided and what condition it is going to be in. Unsuitable donations as in recent Pakistan earthquake [111], or genetically modified food in Southern Africa [160], or expired medication in Armenian earthquake in 1988 [44], are examples of situations where product mix and timing of the donations were not particularly appropriate. Such issues add to the complexity of managing humanitarian logistics.

5.5 Risk Management

Disaster preparedness strategies can be developed using a risk management framework. Paton [122] describes the process of how "incident, operational and organizational demands interact with resilience and vulnerability factors to affect stress risk during mobilization, response and reintegration phases of disaster response". In addition to this perspective, disruption of humanitarian supply chains can also be understood based on the fundamentals of vulnerabilities of supply chain [3, 77, 81, 93, 123].

Two categories of risk affect the design and management of a supply chain; risks due to the lack of coordination between supply and demand, and risks due to a disruption in the supply chain because of natural disasters, economic downturns, and terrorists [77]. The first category, where there are uncertainties of supply as well as demand, was discussed in Section 2.2 ("Supply Chain Perspective"). In the second category where disruption is due to natural disasters the risk management approaches lead to alternative supply chain models. This is described by Papadakis and Ziemba [120] where the authors trace the financial consequences to alternate models of build-to-order as opposed to build-to-stock. Due to global outsourcing and the lead time involved in such supply chains, disasters add to the complexity [78]. Kleindorfer and Saad [77] recommend "Specifying sources of risk and vulnerabilities,

Assessment and Mitigation" as three fundamental tasks that must be "practiced continuously and concurrently" based on four premises of specification of underlying hazard for the risk, quantification of risk through risk assessment process, attention to decision environment, and integration of policies and actions with continuous risk assessment and coordination among supply chain players. These organizational issues can be better understood if we review the case studies. As mentioned earlier through the current practices of case studies we get a better perspective of inadequacies in the current academic research. Additionally, in the next section we also describe the challenges faced by the humanitarian logisticians. Thus the current practices described and challenges faced lead us to suggest the need for future research.

6
Conclusions and Potential for Future Research

In the last two sections we reviewed and discussed research in supply chain issues based on analytical models and we also perused organizational issues in humanitarian logistics. Each of these research articles dealt with important aspects of improving operations during response and relief. One fact that we need to remember is that to maintain or increase the efficiency and effectiveness of the humanitarian logistics, specifics are important but only in the context of the humanitarian space [158]. In this section we first describe some case studies which lead us to challenges faced by current humanitarian agencies. These help us to set the possible agenda for future research. We also outline in this section.

6.1 Examples of Actual Practice

In this section we describe case studies of some recent disasters. These case studies uncover the processes underlying humanitarian logistics, some of the lessons learned, and describe progress made in the last few years by humanitarian organizations in responding to disasters. But equally importantly they also direct us toward the needs of the future research. Analytical models simplify the real-world situations to characterize dynamically complex systems, quantifying the tangible as well as intangible impacts of certain events and identifying the likely outcome [66]. However, the case studies offer a contrast to these by describing the actual practice. We use these case studies of the past and the challenges of today as experienced by the humanitarian officials to set an agenda for research in the field of humanitarian logistics by inspiring the readers to pursue research in this area.

In addition to other lessons learned through these case studies most of the cases suggest the importance of humanitarian space [158] governed by three equally important principles, humanity, neutrality, and impartiality. Humanity implies "that human suffering should be relieved wherever found". Neutrality implies "that relief should be provided without bias or affiliation to a party in the conflict" and impartiality implies that "assistance should be provided without discrimination and with priority given to the most urgent needs".

To understand this aspect of humanitarian logistics in the context of the analytical models and organizational issues discussed in the previous sections consider the following situation. For example, an emergency official needs to evacuate affected population due to a natural disaster from a region that covers two areas, first one is smaller but closer from the temporary collection site and the second is larger but further away from this site. The first area is not as dire in need of evacuation as the second area. First area also has fairly affluent population whereas the second area is economically depressed.

The question is if the official decides to be in the humanitarian space with his limited resources and in face of forecasted further deterioration, which area should he focus on? An analytical model with cost-minimization objective may result in an optimal humanitarian policy of evacuating the first group, it being closer. But this would compromise neutrality and impartiality. Discussion of such questions is critical since a traditional optimization model may address the operational issues but not necessarily the supporting principles. These concerns, in general, have not been adequately addressed in the existing research in the area of humanitarian logistics.

A severe earthquake of magnitude 7.9 on the Richter scale occurred in Gujarat, India in January 2001. International Federation of Red

6.1 Examples of Actual Practice 75

Cross and Red Crescent Societies (IFRC) were the "choreographer" of disaster management. The role of collaboration was critical based on the necessities of the supply chain such as diverse commodities, globalization, and the dynamic nature and the short time span of its existence. IFRC was able to extend help to the affected population in this area using a flexible logistic system, in spite of extreme uncertainties and limited authority. This successful relief effort occurred despite initial lack of information and a distinct shortage of resources throughout the effort [136]. However, this case study uncovers the value of reliable information of the casualties which is necessary to set up the response supply chain.

The need for organization is uncovered in the case study done after the 1999 Armenian earthquake in Colombia [98, 99]. Due to coffee production, and Colombia being the major global provider of coffee, this had lasting effect not only on the home country but also on the whole world.

A sequel to this case study [137] discusses the efforts made by IFRC using their failure to respond promptly to the 1998 Hurricane Mitch disaster that swept through Central America. The case describes five different resources — people, knowledge, goods, money and humanitarian communities — that are essential factors in being prepared for a disaster.

The genesis of United Nations Joint Logistics Centre (UNJLC) lies in response to the 1996–1997 crises in eastern Zaire. The concept evolved until the Afghanistan crisis in 2001 [134]. The case relates how the process of deployment works and highlights the deficiencies as well as the strengths of UNJLC's concept. UNJLC also dealt with operational and logistical bottlenecks during the first six months of the Afghanistan crisis in 2001 [135]. The bottlenecks were transportation (land as well as air), inventory, infrastructure network, and security for all the activities. But collaboration among humanitarian organizations and peace-keeping military forces along with operational issues are also critical to success of response and relief. Continuation of the response by UNJLC during the second year of the Afghanistan crisis led to strategic nation-building initiatives for planning for such crises [133].

In the 2010 earthquake, in Haiti, planes could not leave the airport due to lack of available fuel. They occupied the ground space and for this reason planes carrying the emergency supplies could not land hampering the disaster aid. Fuel is a critical resource in case of disaster. The UNJLC played an important role in fuel availability and supply during the 2003 Iraq crisis. A Fuel Cell is a structure that addresses the availability and sourcing of fuel to the humanitarian community. The case study [92] uncovered the need for a structured process for designing and managing the fuel supply chain. The case points out the importance of prepositioning of this critical yet overlooked commodity, and suggests how a supply chain for such a commodity can be managed. This is an important research area to explore.

Multiple loads of relief supplies arrive usually in the aftermath of a disaster. Humanitarian Supply Management System, SUMA[1] is a tool for managing such relief supplies from the time the donor pledges are made to the time supplies reach the affected population. Tomasini and Van Wassenhove [159] describe the process of implementing SUMA during the earthquakes in El Salvador in 2001. They discuss how the humanitarian operation can be complex due to interactions between various parties in a politicized environment. The issue of humanitarian space is of note here.

The 2002 Southern Africa food crisis in the context of distribution of genetically altered food donations leads to various issues that need to be investigated. The partnering of logistic company with a humanitarian organization for eliminating world hunger points out certain aspects of humanitarian space. Malawi, Lesotho, and Zimbabwe suffered a food shortage from environmental, political, demographic, and economic factors. Much of the food donated was genetically modified, so the food was refused because it was believed by the local population that the lasting impact would be worse than the existing shortages. WFP did its best with the situation, trying to stimulate the local economy and adjust planning to improve the situation. In addition to other lessons learned the case study [160] illustrates the need for a humanitarian relief supply chain to be agile and adaptable.

---

[1] (http://www.disaster-info.net/SUMA/english/WhatisSUMA.htm)

The response and relief situations described so far suggest that resource allocation, bottleneck identification within various services such as transportation, reliable infrastructure networks, designing and managing a fuel supply chain, inventory management of food are topics of interest in humanitarian logistics. In addition to the supply chain issues, organizational issues such as collaboration, information management need to be studied to manage the crises better.

A Hastily Formed Network (HFN) is a formalization of the idea of "quickly forming a team for particular, urgent task, and then disbanding it when done" [34]. An HFN is based on following fundamentals: the network must be established quickly and needs to have players from different communities working together in a "conversation space" so that they can plan and execute the action plan in agreement. In this way, these players are able to fulfill a large and urgent mission [67]. In disasters, an HFN is useful when the advanced networking (electronic) technology can help resolve humanitarian agency issues.

Steckler et al. [148] describe a historical synopsis through a case study of Naval Postgraduate School's (Monterey, United States) deployment of HFN immediately after Hurricane Katrina in the Gulf Coast of Mississippi. The authors provide a step-by-step account of lessons learned and make recommendations for deployment of communications infrastructure for disasters in the future. The case study describes in detail what the network architecture was, how the nodes providing voice and data connectivity to the first responders as well as to the local health facilities, government offices, police, and fire station were located. They also report how this network evolved into PODs and victim shelters. Such research is needed to find innovative solutions to peculiar situations.

A similar case study [67] using HFN describes the United States Naval Station mission to the Caribbean and Central/South America. The study describes how a highly experienced team of ICT experts formed HFN to enable real-time collaboration over the entire area for effective humanitarian relief operations. This case study has a focus that would be of interest and use to those concerned with military support of security, stabilization, transition, and reconstruction in face of a disaster. These cases related to hastily formed networks suggest another area where research will lead to interesting solutions to the issues in disaster response.

Humanitarian logistics in the context of information technology and collaboration [45] among organizations using information communication technology (ICT) is found to be an important and critical issue in organizing a response supply chain. The efficiency of humanitarian organizations can be managed using information technology in the context of IFRC [80]. The authors explain the information flow in the humanitarian supply chain which encompasses the range of activities such as preparedness, assessment through performance evaluation of the information chain.

Farmer and Johnson [45] discuss ICT as a tool for coordination of "relief and development". "NetHope" organization which was founded by information officers of various organizations, humanitarian organizations such as Save the Children, and private companies such as Cisco Systems and Microsoft is cited as an example from different strategic views such as "technology finding hub, software services provider, equipment innovator, procurement service" (provider), networker and educator or "thought leader".

6.2 Challenges Today in Humanitarian Logistics

The survey of published research and research currently underway (as known to the author) has been given as an overview of the type of analytical techniques and tools and organizational framework useful in humanitarian logistics. Case studies have described the on-location and in-field issues of different disaster situations. Interviews with and presentations of individuals involved in disaster response and humanitarian relief have resulted in the following discussion about the challenges faced by and need for research in humanitarian logistics.

Academics can play an important role in addressing these needs to help improve efficiency and effectiveness of preparedness, response, and recovery operations in case of a disaster. Lessons learned thus far from previous disasters have led to considerable thought and analysis among humanitarian logisticians. The issues discussed below are certainly not the only challenges faced by this sector; however, the focus here is from the perspective of operations management and operations research.

After hurricane Katrina, FEMA has established a Logistics Directorate to uncover and then meet those uncovered challenges. The challenges they face are across all the stages of planning, management, and sustainment [143]. They believe that the standardization of systems would improve the relief structure. Moreover, FEMA would benefit from a "comprehensive planning/systems approach to addressing all hazards supply chain management issues of which quantitative analysis is but one tool" [142].

American Red Cross (ARC) faces numerous challenges in their logistics system [121] in the process of responding to natural disasters, preparing communities through education for safety in health, delivering blood, and many such services. The logistics team, more often, ends up reacting as opposed to following a preset process. Due to the fact that every disaster is different, demand varies based on type of disaster. In a situation of multiple disasters there is a possibility of competition of demand. A challenge in the response supply chain is "mixed sourcing of resources". Another issue in their supply chain is the lack of visibility of supplies once they leave the warehouse. Cradle-to-grave visibility needs to be a requirement for all supplies, services, and last but not the least, costs. An important challenge for the material flow of this supply chain is damages and lost physical infrastructure such as roads and communications. Both these agencies, FEMA and ARC, will benefit from a systemic supply chain analysis of response.

Interaction and preferably collaboration between humanitarian organization like ARC and FEMA affects the disaster response [106]. State or local governments also depend on United States Northern Command (NORTHCOM) for assistance and support along the same principles. More research pointing out the compatibility of these organizations, additionally with military, is needed.

ARC focuses on three issues due to their importance in the humanitarian logistics deployment: building capacity at the local level, planning and offering assistance during recovery, and drawing on the knowledge from lessons learned during planning and evacuation.

Managing personnel capacity and assistance from local communities give rise to challenges in assigning right people to right tasks at right time. This can be resolved using well-known modeling techniques.

Another critical planning issue is sheltering. This is a "difficult beast" as characterized by ARC. In addition to the recent research in prepositioning of supplies, research in planning for shelters is needed to identify the location and capacities of the shelters.

International Medical Corps provides vital health care services training for helping people affected by war, natural disasters, and diseases help themselves [68]. The constant need for humanitarian logistics means that long-term development for humanitarian aid, which also translates to more prepositioning and planning for humanitarian logistics, is a necessity. The relief efforts must have greatest impact at the right place and right time. For this the information flow in supply chains must be robust. A priority should be where the data from the preferred supplier are captured, the information is translated into that agency's terms and definitions, and then "e-follow" it through subcontractors (if they exist) to find delivery information. Different agencies involved in humanitarian logistics at different times locate their warehouses and store their supplies. This results in separate warehouses and separate PODs. There needs to be consolidation, at least, of the database of all supplies available on location. Hyde [68] suggests that there is a need for one universal software package that is capable of tracking all available supplies in case of disaster to offer transparency of information and usability to all parties concerned. This is quite a challenge but it is possible with research for achieving this goal.

Daoudi [29] of WFP, a one-stop-shop with virtual stockpile of food (a database explaining inventory of supplies), believes that there needs to be greater "predictability, accountability and partnership" to improve efficiency and effectiveness of humanitarian response. These three aspects can be improved, provided there exist benchmarks and performance measures. At CARE-USA, Gazashvili [52] believes that measuring performance in terms of "timeliness of response", "quality and accountability", and "competence in core sectors" is essential. Defining and establishing such metrics of performance measures and setting benchmarks will add rigor to the lessons learned. It will also provide knowledge and analysis of what worked when. All these translate to the need for more research in collaboration, reliability of food network, reduction of response time, and performance measure for the response supply chain.

At the Bureau for Global Health, USAID, Emrey [41] believes that there exists a need for strong public sector pharmaceutical supply chain that is managed well. Current supply chain systems are multiple and hence complex with diverse sources of supply. This is a challenge for managing inventory and distribution which subsequently dictates more research. Another complication in this supply is counterfeit medicines, which create issues such as contamination and disruption in a supply chain though there exists some research in this field, more is needed.

Listening to emergency planners and first responders and discussing their issues and difficulties bring many questions to a researcher's mind. For example,

- *Unpredictability of the timing* of most of the disasters leads to
    - How can a state of preparedness be maintained?
    - How should the adequate inventory be sustained?
    - How can information about inventory be shared?
    - Is prepositioning the answer?
- *High uncertainty in location* leads to
    - Should partnerships with private sector, that have outfits located all over in the disaster prone areas, be pre-negotiated?
    - What information is available about access and infrastructure?
    - Can economies of scale and scope help mitigate the challenge?
    - How can infrastructure be dealt with for last mile distribution?

- *Variability of demand* in timing as well as quantity during a disaster raises questions such as
    - How can structure for demand be modeled perhaps based on historical data?
    - Will transparency and visibility of information within organization eliminate this problem?
- *Unpredictable supply* lines in a response chain lead to
    - Is virtual stockpile the answer?
    - Where to source, locally or internationally?
    - How should the donations be handled?
        * What about modified or altered food?
        * How about expired medications?
    - What will guarantee smooth supply of critical supplies and services?
        * Is funding available for that?
        * Are contracts in place?
    - What is adequate? What is fair?
- *Speedy response* is critical in case of crisis, hence
    - How can cycle time for relief be reduced?
    - How can critical transportation infrastructure be maintained?
    - How can access to affected areas impact the speed?
    - What can be done to reduce effect of the location on last mile distribution?
- *Prepositioning of assets* may be the key to overcome the first few challenges in anticipation and then actual disaster. In that case,
    - What should be the strategic as well as operational prepositioning?
    - What part of budget should be invested in prepositioning as opposed to reactive response?

- *Objectives* of humanitarian supply chain is focused on response and relief, yet
  - How does one place monetary value on human suffering or life?
  - What should be the performance measures of confirming whether the objective has been achieved?
  - What can be done to achieve a convergence of goals of all the parties?
- *Collaboration* and partnership is a key to successful humanitarian supply chain. In order to accomplish this
  - Why and how should participating sectors prepare for disaster?
  - How can a private sector company, with its main objective of making money, justify involvement in humanitarian logistics?
  - How can competition for the same assets be avoided?
  - How can local communities be involved to help understand cultural, geographical, and political environment?
- One of the major lesson learned from recent history is that humanitarian aid is going to be *perpetual and persistent* in the future. Hence,
  - Can skills be developed for humanitarian operations through training and education?
  - Which sectors would benefit the most from such program?
  - What type of program should be designed?

The above-mentioned issues as well as the challenges faced by various humanitarian logisticians lead to fertile research field researchers will have to build and develop roadways into it with the help of emergency planners and responders. In the next subsection some such opportunities are discussed. Academics know that there is no such thing as a silver bullet or one single methodology, database or software that will solve most of the problems in humanitarian logistics. As Owens [118] put it, "one size does not fit all but it is possible to find a tool from ONE toolbox".

6.3 Future Research

Successful humanitarian logistics involve using "analytical skills to develop and apply tools and techniques to problems in order to structure complex messes" Van Wassenhove [164]. Humanitarian logistics are inherently chaotic and, as discussed before, extremely complex. The complexity can be dealt with if the researchers help meet these challenges through analytical models and systems bearing in mind the unique challenges of this field.

One of the complexities is the location of critical facilities to handle the response or relief. Optimal locations of warehouses and distribution centers for emergency supplies and services, in addition to optimal location of help centers in an effort to evacuate, are some of the challenges in any humanitarian relief or disaster response instances. Such location problems are part of prepositioning of assets and are subject to allocation of resources. There exists a need for research in various aspects of these vital issues. Existing models need to be enhanced and extended. For example, Salmeron and Apte [132] model can be enhanced to incorporate alternate objectives such as the total budget for a desired level of performance of other goals. This concept is universal in commercial logistics and would be significant to incorporate it in humanitarian logistics. Being aware of effects of public policy, ethics and economics is of course necessary here. Another example is the model developed by Cataldi et al. [24] applying system-based approach to allocate resources in Malaria prevention as provided to WHO. This research could be extended to other diseases in other geographic areas bringing critical issues, such as eliminating guesswork and unreliability in deployment of prophylaxis, by adding different sets of constraints and objectives. Such research can be applicable in location of PODs as discussed by Lee et al. [88].

Inventory management is a critical issue in all phases of commercial, military, or humanitarian logistics. From the perspective of preparation in the response, Balcik and Beamon [10] offer a model that provides optimal facility locations for the response supply chain in case of sudden-onset disaster in terms of number of distribution centers and amount of stock of emergency supplies. Numerous extensions of this model can be studied. For example, the assumption made by the authors in offering inventory policy for a single disaster as opposed to multiple occurring simultaneously can be removed and models could be developed for such scenarios.

Another example is where Lodree and Taskin [95] describe a stochastic inventory control for proactive disaster recovery planning. Their model tackles a hurricane event. But this can be integrated for instance, with a sophisticated hurricane prediction model such as one described by Regnier [127]. We believe that stochastic models that incorporate inventory levels for different types of supplies with different lead times and reorder points that share capacities of warehouses or distribution centers in case of disasters of sudden or slow-onset, would benefit the emergency planners substantially.

Research on performance measures of the response supply chain can be found in Beamon [13, 14]. However, it would be useful to extend these concepts further. For example, it would be beneficial to know how the behavior in the humanitarian sector is being driven by which performance measures.

In planning or executing transportation of emergency supplies and service vehicles to the affected population as well as evacuation of the same population, the infrastructure demands close scrutiny. Lack of transportation assets and equally important robust traffic management can hinder extensively in such effort. Though there exist some body of research in transportation and evacuation using multi-commodity, multi-criterion, stochastic network models, these models can render reality if factors, such as public policy and ethics in evacuation of the disabled, and human assessment and knowledge in transportation, are incorporated.

For these existing models, in their enhancements and extensions, there are three extremely important factors that researchers need to keep in mind. First factor is the data used to validate the model. Due to data limitations researchers are forced to estimate certain parameters and input data. Therefore, the models need to be robust to the available data. Frequently, data estimates are done in consultation with emergency planners or persons knowledgeable in the area it would support validity of such implementation and add to the analysis if actual data can be used. Benefits could be gained if such database is created and updated based on disasters events.

Though incorporating "real" data are essential, incorporating reality of the event leads to complex models. Therefore, we believe that the second factor is solution approach for these models. This issue is twofold. First, the complexity of models usually means the use of commercially available optimization software. This increases computational burden and we believe, takes the attention away from managerial consideration. Computational analysis is a vital part of some other fields but humanitarian logistics will benefit more if the focus of the research is on developing models and solving them to "near optimality" and not necessarily to optimality. Therefore, future research should be directed to develop heuristic approaches as well. Secondly, the solution approach that uses sophisticated mainframe-based software may not be as user friendly as desktop-based, easily accessible, and well-known software package such as, for example, Excel. Research being user friendly is critical to its implementation. Hence, we believe developing such solution approaches is important if the research is to be of use to the humanitarian logistics community.

All this analytical approach needs to take place in the humanitarian space as discussed earlier. Research in this newly defined area of humanity, neutrality, and impartiality is critical and essential for forwarding the cause and benefits for humanitarian logistics. In addition to these fundamental factors, another factor that also needs to be part of model development is the concept of fairness.

Finally, as researchers in this area know it is difficult to study situations in humanitarian logistics. Some of the reasons can be attributed to lack of time for participation on behalf of personnel from emergency agencies. This participation is necessary to understand the problem and gather data. Given a situation, developing analytical models is within reach of the academic research. The difficulties arise in collection of data, the critical buy-in from the emergency agencies, long periods of time in doing that and the necessity of interdisciplinary skill set and researchers to carry out the research. Some of the disasters occur in developing countries and hence the response and relief work is carried out in those locations. Access to these countries can pose difficulty. In this case validating the model using real data, communication of implications of the solution to the interested agencies and measuring the effect of such study are critical yet hard to accomplish. Researchers who have been termed successful in such research studies have been able to overcome most of these obstacles by virtue of patience, persistence, and collaboration.

Some of the opportunities for research that will improve efficiency and effectiveness of the humanitarian logistics are listed below. This is by no means an exhaustive list but a beginning of a registry of potential future research topics which is dynamic in nature.

- *Prepositioning:* Facility location, inventory management for speed of distribution, developing user-friendly models
- *Characteristics of the humanitarian supply chain:* visibility versus speed, complexity of existing supply chains versus simplification for distribution, vulnerability to disruption, process cycle time
- *Material flow in a humanitarian supply chain:* stochastic demand, managing supply with uncertainty in scale and scope, complexity due to multiple resources from mixed sources such as stand-by suppliers, last mile distribution
- *People flow in a humanitarian supply chain:* evacuation, clusters of responders, local community capacity
- *Objective of the humanitarian supply chain:* life-saving emergency response versus sustaining long-term developmental aid
- *Performance measures:* definition, establishment
- *Information management:* supply chain network visibility and transparency of source-to-sink flows, common database for on-location provisions across humanitarian agencies
- *Collaboration:* across and within sectors as well as agencies

As students of science and analytics, academics can use their knowledge and skills to develop tools for improving the efficiency and effectiveness of humanitarian logistics — and thus improve disaster and humanitarian responses.

Acknowledgments

First of all I want to express my gratitude to Charles Corbett for the support and guidance throughout the process. I would like to extend my heartfelt thanks to Margaret Brandeau for painstakingly reviewing the very first draft of this article and the anonymous reviewer whose valuable insights improved this article significantly in the latter stages. I am also grateful to Moshe Kress and Javier Salmeron for their comments and suggestions, and numerous scholars who shared their working papers with me. Finally, I would like to thank the publisher for giving me this opportunity.

References

[1] A. Ak, J. L. Heier, C. L. Wardell III, O. Ergun, and P. Keskinocak, "Improving the pan American health organization's vaccine supply chain," poster presentation at Conference on Humanitarian Logistics Conference, H. Milton Stewart School of Industrial and Systems Engineering at Georgia Tech, Atlanta, United States, 2009.

[2] D. Alexander, "Towards the development of standards in emergency management training and education," *Disaster Prevention and Management*, vol. 12, no. 2, pp. 113–123, 2003.

[3] A. Apte, "Fresh produce supply chain: Design and vulnerability," Unpublished research, 2008.

[4] A. Apte and G. Ferrer, "Supply chain for vaccine distribution," Unpublished research, 2009.

[5] A. Apte and S. Heath, "A plan for evacuation of disabled people in the face of a disaster," Unpublished research, 2009.

[6] O. M. Araz, T. Lant, J. Fowler, and M. Jehn, "A pandemic influenza," poster presentation at Conference on Humanitarian Logistics Conference, H. Milton Stewart School of Industrial and Systems Engineering at Georgia Tech, Atlanta, United States, 2009.

[7] S. Aviles, E. Bah, M. Jimenez, L. Li, A. Morales, J. Wade, and O. Ergun, "Supply chain optimization for world food programme," Poster presentation at Conference on Humanitarian Logistics Conference, H. Milton Stewart School of Industrial and Systems Engineering at Georgia Tech, Atlanta, United States, 2009.

[8] D. L. Bakuli and J. M. Smith, "Resource allocation in state-dependent emergency evacuation networks," *European Journal of Operation Research*, vol. 89, pp. 543–555, 1996.

[9] A. Balakrishanan and J. Geunes, "Collaboration and coordination in supply chain management and e-commerce," *Production and Operations Management*, vol. 13, no. 1, pp. 1–2, 2004.

[10] B. Balcik and B. M. Beamon, "Facility location in humanitarian relief," *International Journal of Logistics: Research & Applications*, vol. 11, no. 2, pp. 101–121, 2008.

[11] G. L. Barbarosoglu and Y. Arda, "A two-stage stochastic programming framework for transportation planning in disaster response," *Journal of the Operational Research Society*, vol. 55, pp. 43–53, 2004.

[12] G. L. Barbarosoglu, L. Ozdamar, and A. Cevik, "An interactive approach for hierarchical analysis of helicopter logistics in disaster relief operations," *European Journal of Operational Research*, vol. 140, pp. 118–133, 2002.

[13] B. M. Beamon, "Measuring supply chain performance," *International Journal of Operations & Production Management*, vol. 19, no. 3, no. 3, pp. 275–292, 1999.

[14] B. M. Beamon, "Humanitarian relief chains: Issues and challenges," in *Proceedings of the 34th International Conference on Computers & Industrial Engineering*, pp. 77–82, 2004.

[15] B. M. Beamon and S. A. Kotleba, "Inventory management support systems for emergency humanitarian relief operations in South Sudan," *The International Journal of Logistics Management*, vol. 17, no. 2, pp. 187–212, 2006.

[16] B. M. Beamon and S. A. Kotleba, "Inventory modeling for complex emergencies in humanitarian relief operations," *International Journal of Logistics: Research and Applications*, vol. 9, no. 1, pp. 1–18, 2006b.

[17] T. Boyaci and G. Gallego, "Supply chain coordination in a market with customer service competition," *Production and Operations Management*, vol. 13, no. 1, pp. 3–22, 2004.

[18] J. Bramel and D. Simchi-Levi, "On the effectiveness of set partitioning formulations for the vehicle routing problem," *Operations Research*, vol. 45, pp. 295–301, 1997.

[19] M. L. Brandeau and S. S. Chiu, "An overview of representative problems in location research," *Management Science*, vol. 35, no. 6, pp. 645–674, 1989.

[20] M. L. Brandeau, J. H. McCoy, N. A. Hupert, J. E. Holty, and D. M. Bravata, "Recommendations for modeling disaster responses in public health and medicine: A position paper of the Society for Medical Decision Making," *Medical Decision Making*, vol. 29, pp. 438–460, 2009.

[21] D. M. Bravata, G. S. Zaric, J. C. Holty, M. L. Brandeau, E. R. Wilhelm, K. M. McDonald, and D. K. Owens, "Reducing mortality from anthrax bioterrorism: Strategies for stockpiling and dispensing medical and pharmaceutical supplies," *Biosecurity and Bioterrorism: Biodefense Strategy, Practice, and Science*, vol. 4, no. 3, pp. 244–262, 2006.

[22] G. Brown and W. M. Carlyle, "Optimizing the US Navy's combat logistics force," *Naval Research Logistics*, vol. 55, pp. 800–810, 2008.

[23] J. A. Carbajal, O. Ergun, P. Keskinocak, A. Siddhanthi, and M. Villarreal, "Debris management operations," Poster presentation at Conference on Humanitarian Logistics Conference, H. Milton Stewart School of Industrial and Systems Engineering at Georgia Tech, Atlanta, United States, 2009.

[24] M. Cataldi, C. Cho, C. Guterriez, J. Hull, P. Kim, A. Park, J. Pickering, and J. Swann, "Operations research bites back: Improving malaria interventions in Africa," Unpublished research, 2009.

[25] Y. C. Chiu and H. Zheng, "Real-time mobilization decision for multi-priority emergency response resources and evacuation groups: Model formulation and solution," *Transportation Research: Part E*, vol. 43, pp. 710–736, 2007.

[26] R. Church and C. ReVelle, "The maximal covering location problem," *Papers of the Regional Science Association*, vol. 32, pp. 101–118, 1974.

[27] J. A. Cooke, "Are you ready for the next Katrina?," *Logistics Management*, vol. 44, no. 10, p. 80, October 2005.

[28] J. Dai, S. Wang, and X. Yang, "Computerized support systems for emergency decision making," *Annals of Operations Research*, vol. 51, pp. 315–325, 1994.

[29] A. Daoudi, "The united nations world food programme," Presentation at Conference on Humanitarian Logistics Conference, H. Milton Stewart School of Industrial and Systems Engineering at Georgia Tech, Atlanta, United States, 2009.

[30] J. M. Day, I. Junglas, and L. Silva, "Information flow impediments in disaster relief supply chains," Unpublished research 2009.

[31] B. K. De, D. Herzog, and C. Davila, "Logistics capabilities improvement project of CARE," Poster presentation at Conference on Humanitarian Logistics Conference, H. Milton Stewart School of Industrial and Systems Engineering at Georgia Tech, Atlanta, United States, 2009.

[32] V. DeAngelis, M. Mecoli, C. Nikoi, and G. Storchi, "Multiperiod integrated routing and scheduling of world food programme cargo planes in Angola," *Computers and Operations Research*, vol. 34–36, no. 6, pp. 1601–1615, 2007.

[33] J. Dekle, M. S. Lavieri, E. Martin, H. Emir-Farinas, and R. L. Francis, "A Florida county locates disaster recovery centers," *Interfaces*, vol. 35, no. 2, pp. 133–139, March–April 2005.

[34] P. J. Denning, "Hastily formed networks," Unpublished research, April 2006.

[35] Department of the Army, *Field Manual 100-16: Army Operational Support*. Washington DC: Headquarters, 1995.

[36] S. Duran, M. Gutierrez, and P. Keskinocak, "Pre-positioning of emergency items worldwide for CARE international," Unpublished research, 2008.

[37] P. Eggenhofer, R. K. Huber, B. Katzy, U. Lechner, and S. Richter, "Towards a research agenda for collaborative crisis response management," Poster presentation at Conference on Humanitarian Logistics Conference, H. Milton Stewart School of Industrial and Systems Engineering at Georgia Tech, Atlanta, United States, 2009.

[38] D. P. Eisenman, K. M. Cordasco, S. Asch, J. F. Golden, and D. Glik, "Disaster planning and risk communication with vulnerable communities: Lessons from hurricane Katrina," *American Journal of Public Health*, vol. 97, no. S1, pp. S109–S115, 2007.

[39] A. Ekici, P. Keskinocak, and J. L. Swann, "Modelling influenza pandemic, intervention strategies, and food distribution," under review, *Manufacturing and Service Operations Management*, 2010.

[40] B. Eksioglu, M. Jin, I. Capar, Z. Zhang, and S. D. Eksioglu, "Highway traffic management in incidents of national significance," *Journal of Emergency Management*, vol. 6, no. 1, pp. 23–36, January 2008.

[41] B. Emrey, "Health system strengthening for developing countries," Presentation at Conference on Humanitarian Logistics Conference, H. Milton Stewart School of Industrial and Systems Engineering at Georgia Tech, Atlanta, United States, 2009.

[42] F. G. Engineer, P. Keskinocak, and L. K. Pickering, "Catch-up scheduling for childhood immunization," Unpublished research, 2009.

[43] O. Ergun, J. L. Heier, and J. Swann, "Providing information to improve the performance of decentralized logistics systems," Working Paper, H. Milton Stewart School of Industrial and Systems Engineering, Georgia Institute of Technology, December 2008.

[44] O. Ergun, G. Karakus, P. Keskinocak, J. Swann, and M. Villareal, "Overview of supply chains for humanitarian logistics," Unpublished research, 2009.

[45] B. S. Farmer and E. M. Johnson, "NetHope — Collaborating for the future of relief and development," Case #6-0026, Tuck School of Business at Dartmouth, United States, 2007.

[46] T. Feng and L. R. Keller, "A multiple objective decision analysis for terrorism protection: Potassium iodide distribution in nuclear incidents," *Decision Analysis*, vol. 3, no. 2, pp. 76–93, 2006.

[47] C. H. Fine, "Clockspeed-based strategies for supply chain design," *Production and Operations Management*, vol. 9, no. 3, pp. 213–221, 2000.

[48] M. Fisher, J. H. Hammond, W. Obermeyer, and A. Raman, "Configuring a supply chain to reduce the cost of demand uncertainty," *Production and Operations Management*, vol. 6, no. 3, pp. 211–225, 1997.

[49] J. Fitzsimmons, "A methodology for emergency ambulance deployment," *Management Science*, vol. 19, pp. 627–636, February 1973.

[50] X. Gan, S. P. Sethi, and H. Yan, "Coordination of supply chains with risk-averse agents," *Production and Operations Management*, vol. 13, no. 2, pp. 135–149, 2004.

[51] X. Gan, S. P. Sethi, and H. Yan, "Channel coordination with a risk-neutral supplier and a downside risk-adverse retailer," *Production and Operations Management*, vol. 14, no. 1, no. 1, pp. 80–89, 2005.

[52] D. Gazashvili, "CARE International: Emergency preparedness, response, and recovery," Presentation at Conference on Humanitarian Logistics Conference, H. Milton Stewart School of Industrial and Systems Engineering at Georgia Tech, Atlanta, United States, 2009.

[53] D. E. Gibbons, *Communicable Crises*. Charlotte, NC: Information Age Publishing, 2007.

[54] E. Gralla, J. Goentzel, and C. Fine, "Heuristics for emergency response supply chains," Poster presentation at Conference on Humanitarian Logistics Conference, H. Milton Stewart School of Industrial and Systems Engineering at Georgia Tech, Atlanta, United States, 2009.

[55] J. Griffin, "Logistics of deworming drug distribution in Zambia," Poster presentation at Conference on Humanitarian Logistics Conference, H. Milton Stewart School of Industrial and Systems Engineering at Georgia Tech, Atlanta, United States, 2009.

[56] D. Guha-Sapir, D. Hargitt, and P. Hoyois, "Thirty Years of Natural Disasters 1974–2003: The Numbers," *Centre for Research on the Epidemiology of Disasters*, Brussels, http://www.emdat.be/Documents/Publications/publication_2004_emdat.pdf. Accessed 5/28/09, 2004.

[57] C. Gunes, W. van Hoevey, and S. Tayur, "An analysis of greater Pittsburgh community food bank," Poster presentation at Conference on Humanitarian Logistics Conference, H. Milton Stewart School of Industrial and Systems Engineering at Georgia Tech, Atlanta, United States, 2009.

[58] A. Haghani and S. C. Oh, "Formulation and solution of a multi-commodity, multi-modal network flow model for disaster relief operations," *Transportation Research*, vol. 30, no. 3, pp. 231–250, 1996.

[59] S. Hakimi, "Optimum distribution of switching centers in a communications network and some related graph theoretic problems," *Operations Research*, vol. 13, p. 462, May–June 1965.

[60] T. Hale and C. R. Moberg, "Improving supply chain disaster preparedness: A decision process for secure site location," *International Journal of Physical Distribution & Logistics Management*, vol. 35, no. 3, pp. 195–207, 2005.

[61] R. Halper and S. Raghavan, "Efficient utilization of mobile facilities in humanitarian logistics," Poster presentation at Conference on Humanitarian Logistics Conference, H. Milton Stewart School of Industrial and Systems Engineering at Georgia Tech, Atlanta, United States, 2009.

[62] C. L. Heidtke, "Reducing the gap of pain: A strategy for optimizing federal resource availability in response to major incidents," Master's Thesis, Naval Postgraduate School, Monterey, California, 2007.

[63] J. Holguin-Veras and L. Destro, "Estimating material convergence: Flow of donations for hurricane Katrina," Poster presentation at Conference on Humanitarian Logistics Conference, H. Milton Stewart School of Industrial and Systems Engineering at Georgia Tech, Atlanta, United States, 2009.

[64] J. Holguin-Veras, M. Jaller, S. Ukkusuri, M. Brom, C. Torres, T. Wachtendorf, and B. Brown, "An analysis of the immediate resource requirements after hurricane Katrina: Policy implications for disaster response," Poster presentation at Conference on Humanitarian Logistics Conference, H. Milton Stewart School of Industrial and Systems Engineering at Georgia Tech, Atlanta, United States, 2009.

[65] J. Holguin-Veras, N. Perez, S. Ukkusuri, T. Wachtendorf, and B. Brown, "Emergency logistics issues impacting the response to Katrina: A synthesis and preliminary suggestions for improvement," Poster presentation at Conference on Humanitarian Logistics Conference, H. Milton Stewart School of Industrial and Systems Engineering at Georgia Tech, Atlanta, United States, 2009.

[66] N. Hupert, "CDC's new preparedness modeling initiative: Beyond (and before) crisis response," Presentation at Conference on Humanitarian Logistics Conference, H. Milton Stewart School of Industrial and Systems Engineering at Georgia Tech, Atlanta, United States, 2009.

[67] L. M. Hwee and N. G. Y. Calvin, "An integrated architecture to support hastily formed network," Master's Thesis, Naval Postgraduate School, Monterey, California, 2007.

[68] W. Hyde, "Applied humanitarian logistics," Presentation at Conference on Humanitarian Logistics Conference, H. Milton Stewart School of Industrial and Systems Engineering at Georgia Tech, Atlanta, United States, 2009.

[69] International Committee of Red Cross, http://www.ifrc.org/Docs/pubs/who/at_a_glance-en.pdf. Accessed 5/28/09, 2009.

[70] M. Islam, "Country level supply chain process review in NGO operations," Poster presentation at Conference on Humanitarian Logistics Conference, H. Milton Stewart School of Industrial and Systems Engineering at Georgia Tech, Atlanta, United States, 2009.

[71] A. Iyer, P. McGee, S. Vempala, P. Biswas, and A. Scott, "A web-based system for homeless shelters," Poster presentation at Conference on Humanitarian Logistics Conference, H. Milton Stewart School of Industrial and Systems Engineering at Georgia Tech, Atlanta, United States, 2009.

[72] M. Jin and B. Eksioglu, "Optimal routing of vehicles with communication capabilities in disasters," Unpublished research, 2008.

[73] C. Johnson, "Environmental sustainability at medshare international," Poster presentation at Conference on Humanitarian Logistics Conference, H. Milton Stewart School of Industrial and Systems Engineering at Georgia Tech, Atlanta, United States, 2009.

[74] S. Khan and A. Richter, "Pilot model: Judging alternate modes of dispensing in Los Angeles county," *Interfaces*, vol. 39, pp. 228–240, 2009.

[75] S. Khan and A. Richter, "Using decision analysis to select alternate modes of dispensing — An example from Los Angeles county public health," *Journal of Emergency Management*, vol. March/April, pp. 39–51, 2009.

[76] K. King and J. A. Muckstadt, "Public health emergency supply chain models," Unpublished Research, 2009.

[77] P. R. Kleindorfer and G. H. Saad, "Managing disruption risks in supply chains," *Production & Operations Management*, vol. 14, no. 1, pp. 53–68, 2005.

[78] P. R. Kleindorfer and L. N. Van Wassenhove, "Risk management for global supply chains," in an overview in *The Alliance on Globalizing*, Chapter 12, (H. Gatignon and J. Kimberly, eds.), Cambridge University Press, 2004.

[79] A. Klose and A. Drexl, "Facility location models for distribution system design," *European Journal of Operational Research*, vol. 162, no. 1, pp. 4–29, 2005.

[80] L. Kopczak and E. M. Johnson, "Can heroes be efficient? Information technology at the International Federation of the Red Cross," Case #6-0021, Tuck School of Business at Dartmouth, United States, 2004.

[81] P. Kouvelis and J. Li, "Flexible backup supply and the management of lead-time uncertainty," *Production & Operations Management*, vol. 17, no. 2, pp. 184–199, 2008.

[82] G. Kovacs and K. M. Spens, "Humanitarian logistics in disaster relief operations," *International Journal of Physical Distribution & Logistics Management*, vol. 37, no. 2, pp. 99–114, 2007.

[83] M. Kress, *Operational Logistics: The Art and Science of Sustaining Military Operations*. Boston: Kluwer Academic Publishers, 2002.

[84] O. Kulemeka, "Using the internet to communicate disaster information to individuals with disabilities and chronic illness," Poster presentation at Conference on Humanitarian Logistics Conference, H. Milton Stewart School of Industrial and Systems Engineering at Georgia Tech, Atlanta, United States, 2009.

[85] H. C. Kunreuther and E. O. Michel-Kerjan, *At War With the Weather*. Pennsylvania: The MIT Press, June 2009.

[86] E. K. Lee, S. Maheshwary, J. Mason, and W. Glisson, "Decision support system for mass dispensing of medications for infectious disease outbreaks and bioterrorist attacks," *Annals of Operations Research*, vol. 148, pp. 25–53, 2006.

[87] E. K. Lee, S. Maheshwary, J. Mason, and W. Glisson, "Large-scale dispensing for emergency response to bioterrorism and infectious-disease outbreak," *Interfaces*, vol. 36, no. 6, pp. 591–607, November-December 2006.

[88] E. K. Lee, H. K. Smalley, Y. Zhang, F. Pietz, and B. Benecke, "Facility location and multi-modality mass dispensing strategies and emergency response for biodefense and infectious disease outbreaks," *International Journal on Risk Assessment and Management — Biosecurity Assurance in a Threatening World: Challenges, Explorations, and Breakthroughs*, vol. 12, no. 2/3/4, pp. 311–351, 2009.

[89] H. L. Lee, "Aligning supply chain strategies with products uncertainties," *California Management Review*, vol. 44, no. 3, pp. 105–119, 2002.

[90] H. L. Lee, "The triple-A supply chain," in *Harvard Business Review on Supply Chain Management*, pp. 87–115, Harvard Business School Press, 2006.

[91] M. Levi, P. R. Kleindorfer, and D. J. Wu, "Codifiability, relationship-specific information technology investment, and optimal contracting," *Journal of Management Information Systems*, vol. 20, no. 2, pp. 77–100, 2001.

[92] J. Levins, R. Samii, and L. N. Van Wassenhove, "Fuels: A humanitarian necessity in 2003 post-conflict Iraq; The role of the United Nations joint logistic center," No. 07/2005-5290. INSEAD, Fontainebleau, France, 2005.

[93] C. Li and P. Kouvelis, "Flexible and risk-sharing supply contracts under price uncertainty," *Management Science*, vol. 45, no. 10, pp. 1378–1398, 1999.

[94] C. Liang, C. Wang, H. Luh, and P. Hsu, "Disaster avoidance mechanism for content-delivering service," *Computers & Operations Research*, vol. 36, pp. 27–39, 2009.

[95] E. J. Lodree Jr. and S. Taskin, "Supply chain planning for hurricane response with wind speed information updates," *Computers & Operations Research*, vol. 36, no. 1, pp. 2–15, 2009.

[96] J. I. MacLellan and D. Martell, "Basing airtankers for forest fire control in Ontario," *Operations Research*, vol. 44, no. 5, pp. 677–686, 1996.

[97] V. Marianov and C. ReVelle, "Siting emergency services," in *Facility Location: A Survey of Applications and Methods*, (Z. Drezner, ed.), pp. 199–223, NewYork: Springer-Verlag Inc, 1995.

References

[98] A. P. Martinez, C. E. Mejia, O. Stapleton, and L. N. Van Wassenhove, "Grinding out an effective disaster response in Colombia's coffee region," No. 09/2009-5610. INSEAD, Fontainebleau, France, 2009.

[99] A. P. Martinez, O. Stapleton, and L. N. Van Wassenhove, "Last mile fleet management in humanitarian operations: A case-study based approach," Unpublished research, 2009.

[100] A. P. Martinez and L. N. Van Wassenhove, "Vehicle replacement in the international committee of the red cross," Unpublished research, 2008.

[101] M. Marx, "Coordinating international response to humanitarian crises," Presentation at Conference on Humanitarian Logistics Conference, H. Milton Stewart School of Industrial and Systems Engineering at Georgia Tech, Atlanta, United States, 2009.

[102] B. Maskell, "The age of agile manufacturing," *Supply Chain Management; An International Journal*, vol. 6, no. 1, pp. 5–11, 2001.

[103] J. Mason and M. Washington, "Optimizing staff allocation in large-scale dispensing centers," *Center for Disease Control and Prevention Report*, 2003.

[104] E. L. Maspero and H. W. Ittmann, "The rise of humanitarian logistics," in *Proceedings of the 27th Southern African Transport Conference*, pp. 175–184, July 2008.

[105] V. M. McCall, "Designing and prepositioning humanitarian assistance pack-up kits (HA PUKs) to support pacific fleet emergency relief operations," Master's Thesis, Naval Postgraduate School, Monterey, California, 2006.

[106] B. McCorry, "Intra- and inter-organizational collaboration in disaster planning and long term humanitarian aid," Presentation at Conference on Humanitarian Logistics Conference, H. Milton Stewart School of Industrial and Systems Engineering at Georgia Tech, Atlanta, United States, 2009.

[107] J. H. McCoy, "Humanitarian response: Improving logistics to save lives," *American Journal of Disaster Medicine*, vol. 3, no. 5, pp. 283–293, 2008.

[108] J. H. McCoy, "Three central stockpiles for 33 million beneficiaries: UNHCR's inventory challenge," Poster presentation at Conference on Humanitarian Logistics Conference, H. Milton Stewart School of Industrial and Systems Engineering at Georgia Tech, Atlanta, United States, 2009.

[109] M. Menezes and M. L. Varela, "Analysis of MSF-Spain stock levels for ongoing projects and the option of creating a new distribution center in east Africa," Poster presentation at Conference on Humanitarian Logistics Conference, H. Milton Stewart School of Industrial and Systems Engineering at Georgia Tech, Atlanta, United States, 2009.

[110] K. Moinzadeh and S. Nahmias, "A continuous review model for an inventory system with two supply modes," *Management Science*, vol. 34, pp. 761–773, 1988.

[111] G. Mortensen, Speech at Naval Postgraduate School. Monterey, California, 12 May, 2009.

[112] J. A. Muckstadt, C. Chan, and J. Chen, "A prototype location allocation model for emergency response in an Anthrax attack," Unpublished Research, 2009.

[113] V. G. Narayanan and A. Raman, "Aligning incentives in supply chains," in *Harvard Business Review on Supply Chain Management*, pp. 171–193, Harvard Business School Press, 2006.

[114] P. Nieburg, R. J. Waldman, and D. M. Krumm, "Evacuated populations — Lessons from foreign refugee crises," *The New England Journal of Medicine*, vol. 353, no. 15, pp. 1547–1549, 2005.

[115] R. Oloruntoba and R. Gray, "Humanitarian aid: An agile supply chain?," *Supply Chain Management*, vol. 11, no. 2, pp. 115–120, 2006.

[116] A. Osuntogun, S. Thomas, J. Pitman, S. Basavaraju, B. Mulenga, and S. Vempala, "V2V: Design of a blood flow system," Poster presentation at Conference on Humanitarian Logistics Conference, H. Milton Stewart School of Industrial and Systems Engineering at Georgia Tech, Atlanta, United States, 2009.

[117] S. H. Owen and M. S. Daskin, "Strategic facility location: A review," *European Journal of Operational Research*, vol. 111, pp. 423–447, 1998.

[118] R. C. Owens Jr., "Collaboration in the USAID/DELIVER PROJECT global health and SCMS HIV/AIDS supply chains," presentation at Conference on Humanitarian Logistics Conference, H. Milton Stewart School of Industrial and Systems Engineering at Georgia Tech, Atlanta, United States, 2009.

[119] L. Ozdamar, E. Ekinci, and B. Kucukyazici, "Emergency logistics planning in natural disasters," *Annals of Operations Research*, vol. 129, pp. 217–245, 2004.

[120] I. S. Papadakis and W. T. Ziemba, "Derivative effects of the 1999 earthquake in Taiwan to U. S. personal computer manufacturers," in *Mitigation and Financing Seismic Risks*, (P. R. Kleindorfer and M. R. Sertel, eds.), Kluwer Academic Publishers, 2001.

[121] R. Parnell, "American red cross disaster logistics," Presentation at Conference on Humanitarian Logistics Conference, H. Milton Stewart School of Industrial and Systems Engineering at Georgia Tech, Atlanta, United States, 2009.

[122] D. Paton, "Stress in disaster response: A risk management approach," *Disaster Prevention and Management*, vol. 12, no. 3, pp. 203–209, 2003.

[123] H. Peck, "Drivers of supply chain vulnerability: An integrated framework," *International Journal of Physical Distribution & Logistics Management*, vol. 35, no. 4, pp. 210–232, 2005.

[124] S. J. Pettit and A. K. C. Beresford, "Emergency relief logistic: An evaluation of military, non-military and composite response models," *International Journal of Logistics: Research and Applications*, vol. 8, no. 4, pp. 313–331, 2005.

[125] A. K. Rathi, R. L. Church, and R. S. Solanki, "Allocating resources to support a multicommodity flow with time windows," *Logistics and Transportation Review*, vol. 28, no. 2, no. 2, pp. 167–188, 1992.

[126] C. G. Rawls and M. A. Turnquist, "Pre-positioning of emergency supplies for disaster response," Paper presented at IEEE International Symposium on Technology and Society, New York, NY, 2006.

[127] E. Regnier, "Public evacuation decisions and hurricane track uncertainty," *Management Science*, vol. 54, no. 1, pp. 16–28, January 2008.

[128] E. Regnier and P. A. Harr, "A dynamic decision model applied to hurricane landfall," *Weather and Forecasting*, vol. 21, pp. 764–780, October 2006.

[129] C. ReVelle, D. Bigman, D. Schilling, J. Cohon, and R. Church, "Facility location: A review of context-free and EMS models," *Health Services Research*, vol. 12, no. 2, pp. 129–146, 1977.

[130] C. ReVelle, D. Marks, and J. C. Liebman, "An analysis of private and public sector location models," *Management Science*, vol. 16, no. 11, pp. 692–707, July 1970.

[131] G. H. Saad, "Transformation of supply chain management challenges into business opportunities," Unpublished research, 2003.

[132] J. Salmeron and A. Apte, "Stochastic optimization for natural disaster asset prepositioning," Unpublished research, 2009.

[133] R. Samii and L. N. Van Wassenhove, "Logistics moving the seeds of a brighter future (UNJLC's second year in Afghanistan)," No. 09/2003-5135. INSEAD, Fontainebleau, France, 2003.

[134] R. Samii and L. N. Van Wassenhove, "The United Nations Joint Logistics Centre: The Afghanistan crisis," No. 052003-5092. INSEAD, Fontainebleau, France, 2003.

[135] R. Samii and L. N. Van Wassenhove, "The United Nations Joint Logistics Centre (UNJLC): The Genesis of a Humanitarian Relief Coordination Platform," No. 04/2003-5093. INSEAD, Fontainebleau, France, 2003.

[136] R. Samii, L. N. Van Wassenhove, K. Kumar, and I. Becerra-Fernandez, "Choreographer of disaster management: Preparing for tomorrow's disasters," No. 06/2002-5039 INSEAD, Fontainebleau, France, 2002.

[137] R. Samii, L. N. Van Wassenhove, K. Kumar, and I. Becerra-Fernandez, "Choreographer of disaster management: The Gujarat earthquake," No. 602/046/1. INSEAD, Fontainebleau, France, 2002.

[138] F. Sayyady and S. D. Eksioglu, "Optimizing the use of public transit system during no-notice evacuations of urban areas," Working Paper, Department of Industrial & Systems Engineering, Mississippi State University, June 2008.

[139] J. D. Schindler and R. Radichel, "Decision-support for mass vaccination during a pandemic influenza using agent-based modeling," Poster presentation at Conference on Humanitarian Logistics Conference, H. Milton Stewart School of Industrial and Systems Engineering at Georgia Tech, Atlanta, United States, 2009.

[140] J. B. Sheu, "An emergency logistics distribution approach for quick response to urgent relief demand in disasters," *Transportation Research: Part E*, vol. 43, pp. 687–709, 2007.

[141] E. A. Silver, D. F. Pyke, and R. Peterson, *Decision Systems for Inventory Management and Production Planning*. New York: Wiley, 3rd ed., 1998.

[142] W. Smith, "Logistics transformation," Presentation at Conference on Humanitarian Logistics Conference, H. Milton Stewart School of Industrial and Systems Engineering at Georgia Tech, Atlanta, United States, 2009.

[143] W. Smith, Private communication. 2009.

[144] S. Sotnikov, "Investigating the effects of partnerships on local health departments preparedness," Poster presentation at Conference on Humanitarian Logistics Conference, H. Milton Stewart School of Industrial and Systems Engineering at Georgia Tech, Atlanta, United States, 2009.

[145] G. C. Souza, Z. Zhao, M. Chen, and M. O. Ball, "Coordinating sales and raw material discounts in a global supply chain," *Production and Operations Management*, vol. 13, no. 1, pp. 4–45, 2004.

[146] O. Stapleton, A. P. Martinez, and L. N. Van Wassenhove, "Last mile fleet management in the International Federation of Red Cross and Red Crescent Societies," Unpublished research, 2009.

[147] O. Stapleton, A. P. Martinez, and L. N. V. Wassenhove, "Fleet care: Servicizing in the humanitarian world," No. 09/2009-5631. INSEAD, Fontainebleau, France, 2009.

[148] B. Steckler, B. L. Bradford, and S. Urrea, "Hastily formed networks for complex humanitarian disasters: After action report and lessons learned from the Naval Postgraduate School's response to hurricane Katrina," Naval Postgraduate School, Monterey, California, 2005.

[149] D. Stouffer, "Logistics in humanitarian assistance operations," 2008.

[150] B. C. Tansel, R. L. Francis, and T. J. Lowe, "Location on networks: A survey. Part I: The p-center and p-median problems," *Management Science*, vol. 29, no. 4, pp. 482–497, April 1983.

[151] E. S. Tean, "Optimized positioning of pre-disaster relief force and assets," Master's Thesis, Naval Postgraduate School, Monterey, California, 2006.

[152] The Economist Global Agenda, "Quality over quantity," www.economist.com/PrinterFriendly.cfm?Story_ID=3535065. Accessed 5/28/09, 2005.

[153] A. Thomas, "Humanitarian logistics: Enabling disaster response," Fritz Institute, pp. 15, 2003.

[154] A. Thomas, "Matching recognition with responsibility," *Freight and Logistics*, http://www.fritzinstitute.org/PDFs/InTheNews/2005/ADR_0605.pdf. Accessed 05/29/09, June 21 2005.

[155] A. Thomas and L. R. Kopezak, "Life-saving supply chains: Challenges and path forward," in *Building Supply Chain Excellence in Emerging Economies*, (H. L. Lee and C. Y. Lee, eds.), New York: Springer Science, 2007.

[156] A. Thomas and M. Mizushima, "Logistics training: Necessity or luxury?," *Forced Migration Review*, vol. 22, pp. 60–61, January 2005.

[157] B. Thornton, "Disaster preparedness, response, and post-disaster operations," Presentation at Conference on Humanitarian Logistics Conference, H. Milton Stewart School of Industrial and Systems Engineering at Georgia Tech, Atlanta, United States, 2009.

[158] R. M. Tomasini and L. N. Van Wassenhove, *Humanitarian Logistics*. New York: INSEAD Business Press, 2009.

[159] R. M. Tomasini and L. N. V. Wassenhove, "Coordinating disaster logistics after El Salvador's earthquake using SUMA's humanitarian supply management system," Working Paper No. 10/2003-5145. INSEAD, Fonainebleau, France, 2003.

[160] R. M. Tomasini and L. N. V. Wassenhove, "Genetically modified food donations and the cost of neutrality: Logistics response to the 2002 food crisis in Southern Africa," Working Paper No. 03/2004-5169. INSEAD, Fontainebleau, France, 2004.

[161] C. Toregas, R. Swain, C. ReVelle, and L. Bergman, "The location of emergency service facilities," *Operations Research*, vol. 19, no. 6, pp. 1363–1373, October 1971.

[162] P. A. Trunick, "Logistics when it counts," *Logistics Today*, vol. 46, no. 2, p. 38, 2005.

[163] E. Uzun, N. T. Argon, and S. Ziya, "A mathematical approach to triage in the context of emergency response planning," Poster presentation at Conference on Humanitarian Logistics Conference, H. Milton Stewart School of Industrial and Systems Engineering at Georgia Tech, Atlanta, United States, 2009.

[164] L. N. Van Wassenhove, "Humanitarian aid logistics: Supply chain management in high gear," *Journal of Operational Research Society*, vol. 57, no. 5, pp. 475–489, 2006.

[165] M. H. Whitworth, "Designing the response to an anthrax attack," *Interfaces*, vol. 36, no. 6, pp. 562–568, November/December 2006.

[166] P. Yadav, "Intra- and inter-organizational collaboration in disaster planning and long term humanitarian aid: Perspectives from the architecture for financing global health," Presentation at Conference on Humanitarian Logistics Conference, H. Milton Stewart School of Industrial and Systems Engineering at Georgia Tech, Atlanta, United States, 2009.

[167] W. Yi and L. Ozdamar, "A dynamic logistics coordination model for evacuation and support in disaster response activities," *European Journal of Operational Research*, vol. 179, pp. 1177–1193, 2007.

[168] W. Yushimito, M. Jaller, and S. Ukkusuri, "Application of voronoi based heuristic for facility location in disasters," Poster presentation at Conference on Humanitarian Logistics Conference, H. Milton Stewart School of Industrial and Systems Engineering at Georgia Tech, Atlanta, United States, 2009.